# ECCENTRIC
# GRACES

# ECCENTRIC GRACES

## Eritrea & Ethiopia through the eyes of a traveler

## Julia Stewart

The Red Sea Press, Inc.
*Publishers & Distributors of Third World Books*

11-D Princess Road
Lawrenceville, NJ 08648

RSP

P. O. Box 48
Asmara, ERITREA

# The Red Sea Press, Inc.

*Publishers & Distributors of Third World Books*

11-D Princess Road      **RSP**      P. O. Box 48
Lawrenceville, NJ 08648      Asmara, ERITREA

| | |
|---|---|
| Book design: | Krystal Jackson |
| Cover design: | Jonathan Gullery |
| Illustrations: | Yegizaw Michael |
| Cover and text photos: | Julia Stewart |

**Library of Congress Cataloging-in-Publication Data**

Stewart, Julia.
    Eccentric graces : Eritrea and Ethiopia through the eyes of a traveler / by Julia Stewart.
        p.    cm.
    Includes bibliographical references.
    ISBN 1-56902-100-7. -- ISBN 1-56902-101-5 (pbk.)
    1. Eritrea--Description and travel.    2. Ethiopia--Description and travel.    3. Eritrea--Social life and customs.    4. Ethiopia--Social life and customs.    5. Stewart, Julia--Journeys--Eritrea.
    6. Stewart, Julia--Journeys--Ethiopia.    I. Title.
DT393.34.S74    1998
916.3504'72--dc21                  98-300057
                                         CIP

# Contents

# Author's Note

*If it weren't for myopia,*
*we could see to Ethiopia.*

The people I met in Africa created this story, the people here at home created the need for me to tell it. The principle players in Africa were: in Eritrea Rachel, Samson, Medhani, Amleset and her family, in Ethiopia Jima and Tesfaye, Jonas and his family, and fellow travelers Kate and Sarah. (As I write this in July 1998 it saddens me to note that names of those in Ethiopia had to be changed due to a border conflict between Eritrea and Ethiopia). None of my books have seen completion without valuable input from Todd Schaffer or without Bongo watching from his basket. The same holds true for this book. Special thanks to my cousin Jeff for serving as a layman reader and to Tom Haythornthwaite for proofreading the galleys.

According to one Ethiopian proverb, "To lie about a far country is easy." Sources on Africa are seldom up to date and many of them are contradictory and not entirely accurate. Alas, we work with what is available. These pages contain, to the best of my knowledge, what I know to be true about Eritrea and Ethiopia. The more subjective factors—the way these two countries affected me—will not be exactly the same for any other person, for even the words of my travelling companions were heard by my ears only, the people I encountered along the way are remembered in my mind, brought to life for the reader (it is hoped) through my pen.

There is not one Eritrea, and there is not one Ethiopia. Every country—particularly those in Africa where life can change at lightning speed or as slowly as summer heat—exhibits a different canvas to every person who sees it. On my next visit, I expect both to look different yet again. But, because it is easy to be myopic about a far off country, I urge you to go and see for yourself.

Julia Stewart
Westerville, Ohio
1998

# Prologue

This is a travel narrative about Eritrea, a tiny sun-drenched country along the Red Sea, and Ethiopia, its giant southern neighbor and former colonial overlord. Among the oldest civilizations on earth, these two African countries can boast over 2,000 years of recorded history.

Eritrean and Ethiopian histories interlock, yet still maintain distinctive features. Eritrea's past revolves around foreign incursions and occupation, as well as ongoing trade and cultural mingling with Mediterranean and Arabian worlds. Ethiopian history speaks of imperial glory and dominance, and for great swaths of time isolation, as its Christian kingdoms held out in highland strongholds while Islamic and pagan militaries swirled around them.

Today, both countries, having just emerged from a thirty-year war, are dirt poor. Many citizens live on less than one dollar a day and both nations receive millions of dollars annually in food and development aid. But, with many well-trained professionals among local and exiled populations, rebounding economies, the rule of law, and rich histories and cultures to draw upon, Eritrea and Ethiopia represent the brightest hope for democracy and growth in Africa in the new millennium.

# PART I

# ERITREA

# Historical Background

Eritrea is a "thorny, forlorn splinter of desert-cum-mountain along the Red Sea" wrote John Gunther in his 1955 book *Inside Africa*. Ancient names for this sliver of land included Medri Geez (land of the free), Medri Bahri (land of the sea), and Mareb Mellash (land beyond the river). Not until the nineteenth-century did Italy, its then colonial master, christen it Eritrea; a name derived from the Greek *mare erythraeum* meaning Red Sea.

Funnel-shaped and lying across the Red Sea from the Arabian Peninsula, the country is bordered by the Sudan to the north and west, Ethiopia's Tigray Province to the south, and Djibouti to the southeast. Eritrea covers 48,000 square miles (125,000 square kilometers), making it about the same size as Indiana or England. Considering Africa's immensity—the continent is four times the size of the continental U.S.A.—Eritrea occupies only a dwarfish part of it.

With a climate ranging from arid to semiarid, no permanent rivers, and no sizable lakes, Eritrea is astoundingly dry. The country's dominant natural feature, the primary reason it has been so coveted by other countries, is a 670-mile coastline. While Eritrea's access to Red Sea trade routes and its position as a gateway to the African interior are counted among its blessings, they can also be regarded as an historical curse.

Eritrea's history is a tale of traders, migrants, and invaders. Several thousand years before the birth of Christ, merchant ships from Pharaonic Egypt sailed to Eritrean shores where they were met by coastal chiefs and departed laden with gold, ivory, incense, skins, and slaves. In the first millennium BC, large numbers of war-displaced Sabeans, a people from southwest Arabia (modern-day Yemen) migrated across the Red Sea into Eritrea. The Sabeans brought with them camels, sheep, and horses, as well as their Semitic language (related to Arabic and Hebrew) and the skill of writing.

Several hundred years before the birth of Christ, the Hellenistic Ptolemies conquered Egypt and also gained control of the Eritrean coast, forcing the Sabeans inland. Eventually, the Sabeans built a powerful empire centered around the city of Axum, situated on a plateau in modern Ethiopia's Tigray Province. The Axumite Kingdom monopolized commerce in the region. Its seaport Adulis (today an Eritrean town called Zula) was a trading center for incense, spices, gold dust, gems, ivory, and other goods. It is believed that by the fourth century AD, Axum was the third most important empire in the world.

At its zenith, the Kingdom of Axum stretched from Meroë in Nubia (now the Sudan)—which it destroyed—across the Red Sea into Yemen and down the coast to Somalia. While Axumite subjects spoke Ge'ez, the genesis of several of the major languages heard in Eritrea and Ethiopia today (Tigrinya, Tigre, and Amharic), the ruling elite adopted Greek as its official language. Christianity began to take root in the region in the middle of the fourth century following the fateful stranding in Adulis of a young Syrian named Frumentius who, while a slave in the royal court, converted King Ezana.

In the sixth century, other tribes in the region pushed into the highlands and gained control of the coast, reducing Axum to a small Christian enclave. By the time Arab invaders sacked the port of Adulis in AD 640, Axum's power had already begun a steady decline. Meanwhile, the Bejas, a Cushitic people inhabiting Eritrea since the earliest times, consolidated their power and by AD 750 established five kingdoms that held sway throughout the Middle Ages over most of Eritrea and parts of northeastern Sudan. These kingdoms, which relied largely on the slave trade for wealth, deteriorated by the thirteenth century. For the next few hundred years, Abyssinian chiefs controlled the Eritrean plateau, but never successfully subdued the surrounding lowlands.

In 1517, during the Ottoman Empire's conquest of Egypt, the Turks pushed down the Red Sea coast and occupied Massawa. Several years later the Portuguese arrived in Massawa and battled against the Turks for many years in the name of religion. In 1530, the highlands also entered a period of unrest when the Imam of Harar (a city in eastern Ethiopia) extended his iron fist as far west as Tigray and Eritrea. The Imam's troops destroyed everything in their wake, forcibly converting hundreds of thousands of Christians to Islam.

By 1557, the Turks regained a firm grip on Massawa. While the Turks ruled the Eritrean coastal plains and inland to Keren for more than three hundred years, Tigrayan royalty controlled the highlands. In 1869, the Turks leased Massawa to the Egyptians. The Egyptians, however, withdrew from Eritrea within a decade due to significant military defeats while trying to conquer Ethiopia.

In the late nineteenth century, during "the scramble for Africa," Italy took an interest in Eritrea. A local sultan sold the port of Assab to the Italian government in 1869. In 1885 Italy occupied Massawa, and by 1888 held Keren. Eritrea remained under Italian colonial rule for half a century, until the British defeated Italian troops in Eritrea during World War II. Britain administered Eritrea from 1941 until 1952, at which point Eritrea's fate was once more placed in the hands of outsiders, this time the United Nations.

According to a reference source from the 1950s, "the wishes of the inhabitants were ascertained" before the United Nations General Assembly decided to federate Eritrea under the sovereignty of the Ethiopian crown. However, key observers in the 1940s suggested that probably one hundred percent of the population opposed a full merger with Ethiopia and up to seventy-five percent of Eritreans, given the opportunity, would have voted for independence. Nonetheless, on December 2, 1950, the U.N. General Assembly declared Eritrea an "autonomous unit federated with Ethiopia." *Time* magazine, in an October 13, 1952 issue, reported a joke from that period that called the U.N. decision "a Bolivian concept of a Swiss federation adapted to an African absolute monarchy."

The federation of Eritrea with Ethiopia came into formal existence on September 15, 1952. From day one, Emperor Haile Selassie's regime violated the federal constitution. Eritrea's separate courts were abolished. Arabic and Tigrinya were replaced as official languages by Amharic, which few Eritreans spoke. Industries were closed, dismantled piece by piece, and moved to Ethiopia. Ethiopians were dispatched to Eritrea to fill key administrative posts and Ethiopian settlers started to arrive.

In 1962, Emperor Haile Selassie simply abolished the federal constitution and annexed Eritrea. Theoretically, all Eritrean land became the property of the Emperor. Eritreans, having watched their few remaining freedoms dissipate, were not prepared to accept a backward step into a feudal kingdom. The coals of a thirty-year war of independence, already smoldering, were now lit. Lasting from 1961 to 1991, Eritrea's fight for independence from Ethiopia became Africa's longest continuous modern war.

Eritrean dissent had already taken distinct shape by 1958 when a group of self-imposed exiles formed a coalition called the Eritrean Liberation Movement (ELM) based in Cairo, Egypt. The military fight for freedom began in September 1961 when several key figures from the ELM backed a band of eleven guerilla fighters in hit-

and-run attacks against Ethiopian police stations. This was the origin of the Eritrean Liberation Front (ELF), a group Ethiopians initially downplayed as *shifta* (bandits).

Eritrea's early liberation movement was plagued by infighting and power struggles. In 1970, a progressive-minded group committed to secular nationalism split from the ELF to form the Eritrean People's Liberation Front (EPLF), which would later become the dominant liberation force. Periods of all-out fighting between the ELF and EPLF ensued, specifically from 1972 to 1974 and 1981 to 1982. The end of the first ELF-EPLF internecine war coincided with political changes in Ethiopia, namely the toppling of Emperor Haile Selassie. The second bout of fighting ended with the ELF splintering into smaller groups, some of them joining the EPLF, others going into exile in the Sudan and Arabian countries.

By the 1970s, the so-called "bandits" had grown into an effective guerilla army and gained control of nearly all the countryside and most towns in Eritrea. It had clearly become a people's war, and the people seemed poised to win. But, the tide of the war shifted following the 1974 overthrow of Selassie by a group of Marxist army officers. Recognizing a new member of the communist camp, the Soviet Union and Cuba pumped up to US$12 billion worth of military supplies and advisors into Ethiopia. In 1978, the EPLF was forced to withdraw from most of the countryside and towns it controlled. Dubbed "the strategic withdrawal," the EPLF consolidated its forces in the mountainous Sahel region. Ethiopia had gained a huge advantage in terms of military hardware and boasted the largest standing army in Africa, yet the war largely remained at a stalemate from 1978 to 1986.

According to Robert D. Kaplan in his article "New World Orphan: Eritrea's Sudden Rebirth" in *The New Republic* on June 24, 1991, military and political experts cited the EPLF as one of the most outstanding guerilla armies in the world. Not only did the EPLF fight effectively, but they created a comprehensive, functioning society behind the trenches. Health care networks and famine-relief programs were established. Hospitals with surgical theaters and schools were built into rocky hillsides to avoid overhead detection. Rebels produced their own drugs and medical supplies, school furniture, and textbooks.

By the late 1980s, the EPLF took the offensive and recovered control of several cities and towns. They also started collaborating with the Ethiopian People's Revolutionary Democratic Front (EPRDF), a Tigray-based rebel army simultaneously fighting to liberate Ethiopia from the Marxist regime. Hostilities in Eritrea finally came to an end on May 24, 1991, when the EPLF triumphantly marched into Asmara. A few days later EPRDF troops marched into the Ethiopian capital, Addis Ababa, as dictator Mengistu Haile Mariam fled the country. The war exacted a huge human toll on Eritrea: more than 150,000 Eritreans died (65,000 of them rebel fighters), 10,000 became disabled, and one-third of the country's population was displaced. Every family in Eritrea had been affected by the war, losing loved ones either to martyr's cemeteries or to the safety and opportunity of other lands, and often to both.

May 24 is Eritrea's Independence Day. It was on this day in 1993, exactly two years after their military victory, that Eritreans around the world voted nearly unanimously to become a sovereign state. A constitution has been ratified that will certainly embody democratic institutions. This is where we find Eritrea today: getting its sea legs as Africa's newest independent state.

# Arrival

*Forget history.*
*Men make history,*
*and we have made an*
*independent Eritrea.*

– President Isaias Afwerki

The passengers greeted each other with an ancient grace, bowing slightly and backing away. Their faces broke into wide smiles and they clasped hands. Verbal exchanges were brief, respectful, well rehearsed, and sounded something like "das...dah-nah...dahnah...das." Theirs is a melodic tongue, softer than Arabic, but just as unpenetrable.

An old woman with deep-set eyes entered the airplane cabin dressed in a flowing white handwoven cotton dress with colorful embroidered trim. A matching gauze shawl, a *shamma,* was thrown over her black leather jacket and she wore chunky high-heeled shoes: Abyssinian tradition meets European chic. A flight attendant

11

tenderly directed the woman to her seat and demonstrated how to buckle the seat belt.

A spellbinding perfume filled the cabin air. With hints of musk and frankincense, it was an earthy, biblical smell. One flight attendant in traditional dress bowed her head slightly in a gesture of welcome. She offered me veal or chicken in a voice that wrapped those meats in an appeal I'd never before imagined. I happily took an olive, which at the time I didn't particularly like, because it had been suggested so invitingly. When it was time to land, the attendant leaned over me like a nurturing mother, with that aroma, and gently pulled forward the seat. I am a woman, I thought to myself. How can a man possibly survive the onslaught of their graces?

A little ditty swam around in my head: "In the land of the beautiful, Cleopatra faces grin, with deep-purple lips, over burnt caramel skin," and it finally sank in. I was heading to the land of beautiful people—Eritrea and Ethiopia. My Ethiopian Airlines ticket called our destination "the great unknown yonder," and after spending more than a year sitting at home in Ohio writing non-fiction books, I was ready for some intrigue.

\*   \*   \*

It was a crisp day when the plane landed at the International Airport in Asmara, Eritrea's capital city. Fifty degrees Fahrenheit (ten degrees Celsius) was not exactly the torrid African climate I'd bragged about when leaving America during the Blizzard of '96, but it was a definite improvement. Had I closely read the scant tourist information available on Eritrea, I would have known that Asmara was built on a nearly one-and-a-half-mile-high plateau, and that despite being situated in a sweltering latitude, the city's great height pacifies the sun's heat.

The airport terminal was under construction. Passengers were directed around temporary walls and over half-tiled floors.

One of many men wearing blue uniforms pointed to a concrete slab and said: "This customs."

At the airport bank, a petite woman sat smiling behind a glass divider. She handed me a pen to sign my traveller's check, but it was low on ink.

"The signature doesn't match," the teller said.

"That's because," I noted, "your pen is running out of ink. Anyway, you can see it's me. Here is my passport. It is my signature."

"Give me another check," she demanded.

"But, you see, I have to sign the check in front of the person who cashes it, so I must give this one to you."

I was perplexed. A frustrating scene echoing the diner episode in *Five Easy Pieces* ensued. The teller finally called over a man with some sort of reconciliatory capacity. He explained that the cashier feared the consequences should her superiors refuse to accept the check because of mismatched signatures. I pulled out one of my own pens and signed another check.

\*   \*   \*

That evening, in the lobby of the Keren Hotel where I was staying, people made themselves comfortable in striped red, black, and khaki stuffed sofas and chairs. The chattering guests—Africans, Germans, French, Brits, Americans, and a lone Filipino—sipped beers and cappuccinos. With amiable expressions and weather-worn faces, most looked like hardened aid workers. The Eritrean customers brought a certain serenity to the din, carrying on quiet conversations dotted with wispy "ts" and guttural "a" sounds. It was as if the room was full of people taking turns using the word "tsetse" in conversation.

The waiter—elderly, jet-black and with a slightly protruding lower lip—wore a white chef's jacket and navy polyester pants cut a tad too short. With cropped, straight hair graying around the edges, he moved at a measured pace. There was no scurrying around madly, no gratuitous cheerfulness. The hotel bar, like the city around it, exuded an aura of calm.

It was only a few years earlier, in 1991, that Asmara was the epicenter of the final throws of Eritrea's war of independence from neighboring Ethiopia. The war had been waging for thirty years—longer than the majority of Eritreans had been alive. It was the most protracted war in modern Africa and, at its peak, pitted a force of 95,000 Eritrean rebels against Africa's largest standing army. Of 300,000 Ethiopian troops, nearly half were stationed in Asmara. While the Eritreans fought mostly with captured weapons, the Ethiopian army was backed by hundreds of millions of dollars worth of U.S. military support until the 1970s, and thereafter by over twelve billion dollars in military aid from the Soviet Bloc.

Although Asmara was spared the carpet bombing that occurred in much of the rest of the country, it suffered in its own way. The effect of the conflict became acute in Asmara in 1975 when the rebels, controlling most of the surrounding villages, commenced assaults on Ethiopian troops in the city. At night, city dwellers could hear the sounds of automatic weapon fire and cannon blasts; they called it *la musica della notte.* The horrors had already begun to mount. In December of the previous year, young Eritreans disappeared in the night, only to be found later killed—victims of "piano wire stranglings." In June 1975, seven young women at a gathering were kidnapped in broad daylight by Ethiopian troops and later raped, mutilated, and shot dead. Eritrean People's Liberation Front (EPLF) sympathizers were rounded up, interned, and many were killed. In 1975 alone, the population of Asmara dropped from 250,000 to 175,000. Young people were sent away for fear of forced conscription into the Ethiopian army and to avert the daily cruelties of occupation. I read of one particular father who drove his teenage daughter to the southern port of Assab from where she walked to asylum in Djibouti. The majority of exiles walked, some for hundreds of miles, to the Sudan.

It was around this time, following Ethiopia's overnight transmutation from feudal empire to Marxist dictatorship, that the tide of the war changed. Faced with the magnified fire-power of a now Soviet-backed Ethiopian army, rebel positions dropped back into the mountains far from Asmara. While the country trudged through another decade and a half of war, residents of Asmara lived like prisoners. "You couldn't even say the word Eritrea," explained one shopkeeper, according to Marguerite Michaels in her July 15, 1991, *Time* article, "Horn of Africa: Tough Terms for a Divorce." Civilians were arrested for just listening to the rebel's radio station. With the decline of Ethiopia's Marxist regime in the late 1980s, the Ethiopian army's position also weakened, and the EPLF eventually regained lost territory.

Eritrean land had been occupied by outsiders almost continually for four hundred years. In the sixteenth century, the Ottoman Turks captured Eritrea's coastline and inland to Keren and controlled it for three centuries. When the Turks finally left in 1848, the Egyptians stepped in. The Egyptians rapidly lost interest, but the Italians had their eye on this prime piece of Red Sea real estate and colonized it from 1886 to 1941. The British came next as administrators of a defeated Italy's colonial territories. When Britain felt obliged to rid herself of difficult overseas holdings, the United Nations was charged with determining Eritrea's fate. This world body turned Eritrea over to its most brutal and oppressive ruler to date—Ethiopia. Finally, the war against Ethiopia was almost won.

It was at 10:00 a.m. on May 24, 1991 that Asmara residents realized EPLF fighters had entered their city. In a spontaneous outburst of happiness and relief, Asmarinos flung open their doors and rushed into the streets to dance in jubilation, some still in their pajamas. The dancing lasted for weeks. On May 24, 1993, exactly two years later to the day, Eritreans around the world, including balloting in forty-eight cities in North America, voted 99.6% for an independent Eritrea. Eritrea's new flag of green, red, and blue triangles with a gold wreath around an olive branch was raised for the first time in Asmara. According to a *Facts on File World News Digest* article, "Eritrea: Independence Declared," dated May 27, 1993, President Isaias Afwerki called it "a moment of joy and resurrection for Eritrea."

*　*　*

The door of the Keren Hotel squeaked open as an Eritrean couple emerged from the dusky streets. Their wide brown eyes scanned the room for an available seat as they nodded polite hellos to other guests. The couple passed under the grand archways, their forms silhouetted against formidable walls covered in tiny green ceramic tiles. Tourism posters showing Eritrean tribespeople and local scenery adorned the walls, as they would in restaurants and hotels throughout Eritrea and Ethiopia.

Colorful plastic streamers over an open doorway drew my attention to the orange-hued dining room. Inside, an ornate column and steel brocade on the walls was covered in thick layers of white paint that spoke of one hundred years of feast and famine. A massive antique sideboard was hidden in the shadows in a back room, like the odd bits and pieces of antique veneer furniture resting in cubby holes and hallways upstairs. One got the impression that the smaller antique pieces disappeared long ago. The tables were set with linen table cloths and napkins, and the plaster was cracking on the tangerine walls, creating an elegant "distressed" look that trendy restaurants in the United States pay liberal sums to achieve.

"Shall I mix-ed it for you?" the waitress asked. She proceeded to conjure up a delectable green salad, brimming with onions and slices of cherry tomatoes, lathered in oil and pepper. It was accompanied by a fresh, tasty loaf of bread unlike any I'd eaten anywhere in Africa.

Eritrea effectively embraces two national cuisines. The region's staple food is *injera*, a spongy, sour-tasting oversized pancake topped with *zigni*, spicy stews of meat, fish, or vegetables, and with pureed legumes and salads. *Injera* is a fermented bread made from *taff*, wheat, or sorghum. *Taff* is an indigenous millet-like grain hailed as a miracle food due to its high mineral content and low-fat, high-protein, high-complex carbohydrate makeup. It is also the only grain which, like grapes, has symbiotic yeast, making it self rising.

The second national cuisine, adopted with gusto, is Italian. "Asmara is a heaven," wrote Philip M. Allen and Aaron Segal in 1973 in *The Traveler's Africa*, "for those who like Italian cuisine." Stay for long and you'll have pasta and pizza coming out your ears. But even Italian food cannot escape Eritrean influence; the spices in the Keren Hotel's marinara sauce made my lips tingle.

My immediate impression was that the Eritreans had created an entire culture on one quality—serenity. The music wafting through the dining room was satiny and melodic (I didn't realize at the time that it was Amharic, not traditional Eritrean music). Peoples' voices resembled crickets chirping at night and their public manners reflected politeness and poise. I was quickly absorbed in the lull.

The atmosphere reminded me of the transformation children underwent at an international youth camp in Virginia where I once worked. The camp banned meat and sugar from everyone's diet. The first day the cafeteria rocked with childrens' clattering voices. By the third day, without their stimulant foods, the children were significantly calmer and more relaxed. It took me not three days, like the children, but only several hours to downshift my system to this Red Sea country's pace. Two well-groomed British couples—I surmised they were World Bank or consulate officials—entered the orange room. Their booming laughter and penetrating high-pitched voices bounced off the cracked walls and cavernous ceilings, breaking my campfire dreams.

"Is there a place I can get some coffee?" I asked the manager of the Keren Hotel. I'm not a habitual after-dinner coffee drinker, but this is coffee country. Coffee is native to Africa and accounts for sixty percent of Ethiopia's foreign currency earnings. The word coffee itself is believed to derive from the name Kaffa, a region in southwestern Ethiopia that remains the country's largest coffee-producing area.

With dark glasses, long curly hair, ruddy skin, and dressed in an unbecoming suit, the manager could be described as "slick" in America.

"You don't like our coffee?" he asked.

He seemed offended.

"Yes, it's fine," I replied, "but I'd like to go outside for awhile."

Saying, "I understand," the manager walked me out front of the hotel onto the Fiat-lined street and pointed toward Bar Vittoria, one of the city's oldest cafes. As is common in other parts of Africa, people don't know street names, which can make taking directions a chore. The Keren Hotel manager, for example, could not even tell me the name of the street directly in front of the hotel.

"I've only been here six months," he said, as if that explained everything.

"Can I walk at night?" I asked.

Looking very unsure why I had asked, he replied, "You can walk until tomorrow morning."

The Bar Vittoria peddles cappuccino, gelato, and Campari. Stenciled across its mirrored walls are advertisements for *vini-liquori-aperitivi-sciroppi-fenili-campari.* Candy jars line the shelves and plastic bags full of cookies are mounded in a glass display case. The pretty cashier sat quietly, elevated in a booth surrounded by smokey glass. As elsewhere in Africa, strangers share tables when space is tight, so I sat beside a lone man. All the customers were male, except me. A snotty-nosed beggar girl followed me into the bar but was quickly shooed away by a waiter.

Back on the streets another urchin with fuzzy hair and streams of tears rolling down his cheeks appeared in front of me. With swollen fingers he carried a plastic tub of roasted peanuts. The tears quickly dried up at the sight of a potential customer.

"Money?" he asked.

"How much?" I said.

"One birr."

I ducked into a photo shop to get some change. No matter where you go in Africa, it never fails that abject poverty gets slapped in your face. I have seen some visitors taking on a Mother Teresa role, giving generously to every downtrodden soul in their path. Others prefer to pick and choose, donating only to those they can easily ascertain as needy, such as lepers, the blind, or the lame. A few manage to ignore it. But in one way or another, you are forced to react. My responses vary, but rarely do I hesitate to buy from diminutive sidewalk merchants, even if I have no need for their wares. I'm obsessed with supporting free enterprise and the notion that self-help is the best help.

The next people to cross my path snuck up quite deliberately from behind.

"Are you enjoying yourself here?" asked one of two handsome Eritrean men, speaking in perfect American English.

"Yes," I replied. "Very much. You're American?"

"No," he replied. "I'm from Canada."

"Well then," I said, aware of Canadian sensitivity to being overshadowed by their more gregarious southern neighbors, "I suppose you should be offended."

A hearty laugh escaped from behind his brilliant white teeth. Samson and his friend Medhani invited me to walk with them through the city's streets, and my first night in Asmara began in earnest.

Throngs of Eritreans promenaded up and down Liberation Avenue. This winsome palm-fringed thoroughfare was formerly called Haile Selassie Avenue, until Emperor Selassie was deposed, and then National Avenue under Ethiopia's Marxist regime. Residents wove through side streets that housed restaurants, cafes, jewelry stores, and sundry shops.

19

*Palm-lined mainstreet of Asmara*

*An Asmara street*

Young boys straddled bicycles, while their older brothers and fathers filed into seedy bars. Like mushrooms, photo shops popped up everywhere. Women strolled arm and arm, while men walked hand in hand.

"They don't know about these things," excused Samson in reference to Western homophobia.

Although the January evening air was quite cool, the thick leather jackets worn by some, including Samson and Medhani, seemed excessive. The three of us chatted furiously as we rambled down the streets. We discussed potential business opportunities in Eritrea, a familiar topic of conversation in a newly independent country. I threw out the idea of a sports club.

"Look at everyone," said Samson. He laughed and motioned with a sweep of his arms toward the lean people on the sidewalks. "They're so thin; no need for a Stairmaster here!"

Eritreans walk everywhere and eat moderately. They don't drink much milk, like in Holland, Medhani's adopted home, where, he said, milk is called "white water." Neither do Eritreans suck down soft drinks the way, for instance, Kenyans and Americans do. Eritrean drinks of choice are coffee, tea, and mineral water.

Upon mentioning that I had heard there was a bowling alley in Asmara, we hopped into Samson's rickety yellow rental car and drove off in search of this unusual amusement. Asmara is a compact city and is easy to get around by foot or taxi. Samson and Medhani had rented the car not for moving around Asmara—although they were enjoying it like a pair of teenagers who had stolen their parents' wheels—but for a weekend trip to the coast. I mulled over an invitation to join them, but concluded with some regret that I needed to reserve Massawa for impending travels with my friend Kate who would be arriving in Eritrea in a few days. The building that once housed the bowling alley appeared before us. Whether the bowling alley still existed or not we were unsure; it looked like a backstreet warehouse shut up tight for the evening.

We entered a bar where they played the music a few decibels too loud, a strange Eritrean affliction. This prevented Medhani, whose English was weak, from effectively entering the conversation. I ordered Zebib, a locally-made anise-flavored liquor similar to Ouzo, causing my new friends to chuckle. I am like their mothers, they said. Older women apparently like to pull out the Zebib bottle for any special occasion, even ones occurring early in the morning, and especially after the birth of a baby. Samson and Medhani ordered Melotti beer: two of the sixty million bottles turned out each year by Eritrea's fifty-seven-year old Asmara Brewery.

In the dozen years that Samson had lived in Canada this was his first trip back to Eritrea. Medhani, Samson's boyhood chum, had lived as long in Holland and was also making his maiden re-entry to the land of his birth. Many young Eritreans, like Samson and Medhani, had been sent away as children, before they could be drafted or abused by Ethiopian troops occupying their city. There are only 3.5 million Eritreans in the world, of which nearly one third live outside the country. A half million remain as refugees in the Sudan, and another 250,000 are scattered across the globe in places as far flung as Australia, Scandinavia, Canada, and the United States. Of the latter group, some are exiled closer to home in countries such as Saudi Arabia (approximately 100,000 live there), Egypt, Kenya, and Ethiopia. So Eritrean "visitors" to Asmara are common.

Samson and Medhani, both staying in Eritrea for a month, had reconnected after all these years by the unfortunate news of the death of Samson's father. The two men had been reviewing their childhood story by story, laughing at each other until their sides ached. The first story they shared with me involved a girl from their old neighborhood who didn't like Samson. The two boys, as I understood it, teased her relentlessly. One day this girl was sitting outside with curlers in her hair. The two boys slung English names at her that she couldn't understand. In a blind fury she yanked the curlers out of her hair and ran off with her hair sticking out in all directions.

They also recalled a day when Medhani didn't come home when he was supposed to paint his house. Meanwhile, Samson had stopped over looking for him. While he waited for Medhani's return, Samson completed the painting job. As Samson sat down before some porridge prepared for him by Medhani's sister, in blew her errant brother. Medhani told a fabulous story about how he'd been arrested by the Ethiopians and knocked around. Samson and Medhani's sister felt so sorry for him that they offered him some of the food. Some days later Medhani confessed to his bare-faced lie. These are the type of tales that might be finished by an American with the statement "you had to be there," but which nonetheless reflect the Spanky-and-Our-Gang charm of Eritrean childhood.

We moved on to Bar Adulis, a quieter place where we could all talk. The room was filled with Art Deco metal chairs and tables, and pictures were strewn high up on the walls, including one of a buxom white woman in a bathing suit. The bar was raised up on a platform, giving the female workers a more commanding post. The barwomen came to our table and greeted us with baby-soft handshakes.

"They respect us," explained Medhani.

"They can smell money," sneered Samson. Medhani wrinkled his forehead in protest.

The owner was a petite yellow-skinned woman with doe eyes and pouting lips. She wore a white sweater with a big faux fur collar, had a pretty face and delicate hands, but possessed the air of a Wild West saloon madame. She proved as hardy as she looked when a drunk patron refused to pay for his liquor. A ruckus broke out. There was arguing and some shoving near the doorway draped with hippie beads. The lone man tried his best to escape into the night, but four barwomen had hold of him and were berating him mercilessly.

"Taxi!" they yelled, slinging that epithet as their most brutal weapon.

The man was a taxi driver, and they quite successfully belittled his occupation. The petite matron wanted an all-out fight with "Taxi," but he finally managed to slip away.

The matron returned to our table and sat for awhile, leaning close to Medhani's bulking frame. He bought her a whiskey, and she recounted the story of the fight with fire in her eyes. She waved her dainty hands freely as she talked in Tigrinya, cupping them to her breasts and then opening them outward again like palm fronds.

"I don't know about in her country," she said in Tigrinya and smiled toward me, "but here she seems nice."

Tigrinya is a throaty language, full of guttural sounds my ears, let alone my mouth, could barely get around.

"You'll get sick if you try to speak Tigrinya," Samson said and they all laughed. "Or spit in your food while talking," he added.

A lunatic poked his head into the bar. The man's eyes darted in opposite directions until he zeroed in on the visitors. He took our hands, each of us in turn, and kissed the back of them with a wet mouth. Through a cock-eyed vacant stare, the scrawny man particularly admired Samson and insisted that Samson kiss his hand in return. Samson did and gave the man some birr in hopes of getting rid of him. Rather than leaving, the deranged man fawned over his benefactor. He kissed Samson's cheek, then the back of his head at which point he drooled down the back of his shirt. I could see Samson's Canadianness overpowering his Eritreanness: he shoved the man away.

Our crazy chum reappeared around midnight. Several workers informed him that the bar was shutting, but he refused to leave and, once more, focused wandering eyes on us. The matron grabbed a tuft of nappy hair at his forehead, yanked him through the bead curtain, and pulled him into the street. The man plunged to the sidewalk, wrapped his body around her slender ankles and took a bite of her foot. She screamed rather from shock than pain. Minutes later the man barged inside again, dropped to the floor and began to flail his legs against the bar.

"Very close to nature in Africa," observed Samson. This was our cue to exit.

The streets of Asmara were now empty. Samson and I waited in the rental car while Medhani ran back inside Bar Adulis to use the restroom. Samson confided to me that his father, having witnessed too many failed cross-cultural marriages, ordered that he must marry an Eritrean. His father's argument stood on two points: first, being Catholic, he was strongly opposed to divorce; second, he was expecting that Samson and his family would return to Eritrea one day. The recent death of his father released Samson from this obligation, but he acknowledged his generation was in a predicament. Samson had lived in Canada for over a dozen highly impressionable years. He said he related better now to Western women than to Eritrean women, particularly those who have never left their country.

Although Eritrean women fought alongside men in the trenches during the war—one-third of guerilla fighters were female—sexist attitudes still linger. The patriarchal nature of Eritrean traditional society is exposed by the local proverb, "Just as there is no donkey with horns, so there is no woman with brains." In many rural areas girls are still viewed primarily as essential laborers for the home and farm and are kept from school. Marriages, routinely arranged by a girl's family, involve large dowries. Polygamy and female circumcision still exist. At times, female fighters who have returned to home villages have been considered unmarriageable because of their independent, nontraditional ways. Women may not be equally represented in the army's top brass and the ruling elit, but it is worth noting that of forty-two members appointed to the Constitutional Commission established in April 1994 twenty were women. And women do hold several senior positions in the government.

A lone bar worker walked briskly past the car. She saw us inside, doubled back, reached in to shake our hands and to say a kind word of farewell, then scurried back around the corner toward home.

"Tell me," Samson turned to me and said. "What kind of courage does it take for you to travel alone like this?"

By this time my new friend's words were slurring, so I didn't feel like squandering the effort to explain. But I knew the answer. It was not about courage at all. Fear was the overriding principle: fear of not doing the one thing I knew I was good at, and that which I realized most others could not do. Family and career obligations prevent most people I know from uprooting themselves and gallivanting around foreign countries. But I am never sure whether many of them would wander off anyway, even if handed the opportunity on a silver platter. In fact, Samson's question exposed some personal concerns I was having about this trip. A person needed a purpose, I thought, a direction. Wandering around aimlessly is just loitering, and a soul can get confused.

By and by Samson and I needed to use the facilities, so we also returned to Bar Adulis. Somehow, at the last minute, Medhani and the bar matron discovered that they had attended grade school together.

"I got taller," he explained, "and she got shorter." I squatted as far as possible above the dirty toilet. The room reeked of urine and ammonia splattered on the floor, and I was feeling claustrophobic.

I heard Medhani cry toward the bathroom door, "The police are here. You are going to get arrested!"

Perfect. First night in Eritrea and I'm headed for the slammer. I dropped my long skirt and dashed out of the restroom and, ducking under a half-closed metal security door, slipped out of the bar. A police cruiser parked outside. As we drove around the corner back to the Keren Hotel, Medhani admitted that the bar owner was actually quite friendly with the police. The mischievous little boy of Samson's stories told earlier in the evening had returned.

My first night back on the continent, I realized that I had forgotten several idiosyncrasies of Africa. For instance, I had planned to have an early-bird dinner before exploring the town, forgetting that hotel restaurants usually operate only during brief set hours. I had neglected to stuff squares of toilet paper in my pockets, knowing that this commodity is a rare find in public places. Most significantly, I had forgotten that in Africa you don't remain alone for very long.

# Asmara

*Our freedom was so expensive. If this isn't going to be a country we can be proud of, then it was all a waste of time.*

— Hagos Ghebrehiwet,
   top official of the People's
   Front for Democracy and
   Justice (PFDJ)

Two well-dressed eight-year-old boys, weaving through cars parked along Liberation Avenue, hurled banana peels at a pair of poorer boys. One of the targets rubbed his forehead where he had been hit; a distressed look swept across his face. An elderly man arrived on the scene, but only in time to see banana peels—incriminating evidence—at the feet of the poorer lads. The old man scolded the victims and ordered them to pick up their rubbish. The boys bent over, meekly protesting, and cleaned up the mess. As I was watching this vignette of

Asmara street life several flashily attired teenagers walked by.

One of the girls smiled and said, "Hi, honey!"

I screwed up my face, "Honey?"

They all laughed the waggish laugh of teenagers throughout the world.

In the dirt courtyard of a vast apartment building with cracked windows and rusted shutters, four little girls jumped rope. The girls eagerly waved hello. I entered the fenced compound and appealed to them with hand gestures to turn the rope high. Surprising myself as much as them, I leaped into the twirling rope and managed several hops and showy twists before my foot got tangled. The altitude hit me hard.

"Whew, I am old and tired," I told the girls in a language they didn't understand, and left them giggling.

Further on, two small boys walked down the sidewalk holding thick chunks of jagged amber glass up to their eyes—a child's version of a psychedelic experience. Teenage boys and girls[1] in matching blue sweaters stood on the steps of a blue school building, gaily prattling.

A horse-drawn carriage rattled across an intersection; a woman snuggled in a shawl while a man held the reigns. Handpainted across the back of the wooden buggy were the words: "Pray to One God Only."

Life unfolds in front of your eyes in Asmara, an elegant city of 400,000. Residents socialize openly and play on the streets. Women in flowing white dresses chat and stroll, their hair worked into buns, French twists, and Shirley Temple curls. Some sport the traditional Tigrinya *kuno* hairstyle: microbraids hugging their skulls down to the nape of the neck where the ends frizz out like a fur collar. Their smiles are like those of toothpaste commercials. To make their teeth appear whiter, Abyssinian women tatoo their gums using thorns dipped in charcoal dye.

---

[1]Those children were fortunate: according to UNESCO figures for 1990-1995, less than twenty percent of Eritrean children were enrolled in secondary school.

Particularly striking are the children with their storybook appearances. There stands Pippi Longstocking, her braids akimbo. On the curb sits a miniature Rastafarian with head sprouting soft dreadlocks. A barefoot boy steps out of a grocery clutching three fresh loaves of bread, a tuft of hair spilling over his forehead as if a castmember of *American Graffiti*. Children tug one another's jackets and lean against each other on benches. Roaming in tot packs, they poke their heads into cafes and bars, twirl balls made from paper and string, and slug each other in the arm. One threesome swatted a ball dangling from a zebra-striped sign pole—homemade tetherball. Almost always the children have something to say about, or to, the tourist.

A grandfather held a small boy's hand while walking down Liberation Avenue. Oblivious to everything else, the boy licked a swiftly melting ice cream cone as it dribbled down the front of his shirt. Asmara's old men, like its youth, could also be featured in children's books. The men wear thick-rimmed black glasses and delightful wool berets. They don soft v-neck sweaters under smart blazers, and wield canes more for style than necessity. They ride bikes and shuffle in and out of cafes and bars, sharing an espresso or a cognac with friends. Reminiscent of the little boys roaming the streets, the old men hold each others hands, pull each other into shops, and tease one other—life goes full circle.

The name Asmara is derived from *arba'ete asmara* meaning "they unite the four." According to local legend, the women of four warring villages on the *Kebessa* Plateau came together and devised a plan to stop the fighting, uniting the villages into one large community.

Walking around Asmara, or Piccola Roma and Secondo Milano as it has been called, is like strolling through the movie set of a romantic bygone era. The city was built in the first half of the twentieth century while Eritrea was an Italian colony. Asmara's architectural leitmotif is Art Deco, a functional style popular in the 1920s and 1930s featuring geometric shapes and bold colors.

From my hotel window, gazing out over flat rooftops where laundry dries under a crystalline blue sky, I detected traces of Zanzibar too. At dusk, a muezzin from a distant mosque formed a soft, trumpeting sound around the words *Allahu Ahkbar.* The muezzin held the note until his lungs gave out. Asmara is a fusion of cultures and epochs: mosques mingle with churches, cappuccino machines with charcoal stoves, taxis and buses with horse-drawn buggies, Korean-built high-rise apartments with 1970s bungalows, computer stores with street corner shoeshiners.

Only steps away from Asmara's palmy main thoroughfare, Liberation Avenue, one finds up-market residential areas graced by elegant Italianate villas with darling Romeo and Juliet balconies. Even the villas' high perimeter walls beg for a picture—stones painted black with contrasting white mortar and radiant bougainvillaea draping over the sides. Sidewalks are made of patterned paving tiles, although much of it crumbled and broken.

Asmarinos sling multilingual greetings with ease— *selam, merhaba, buon giorno, hello.* Shop owners also tout their wares in many languages. The lingering use of Italian on shop signs, like *La Ferramenta* and *Farmacia,* serve as reminders of the large Italian community that once resided in Asmara. Toward the end of the nineteenth century, hundreds of thousands of Italian peasants settled in Eritrea. Some 70,000 Italians still remained in Eritrea at the end of Italian colonial rule in 1941. But by the 1970s, Eritrea had fallen under Ethiopian communist occupation and only a few hundred remained. Many older Asmarinos still converse in Italian and all Asmarinos pepper their speech with Italian words: *allora* (then), *bicchiere* (glass), and *andiamo* (let's go) jump out of sentences.

Whereas Tigrinya and Arabic are the most widely spoken languages in the country, English is now the language of instruction in secondary schools and is fast becoming the foreign language of choice. The majority of people I encountered in Asmara spoke Tigrinya—one of the nine indigenous languages of Eritrea. I was able to make out a few Tigrinya words because of my knowledge of Kiswahili. Both languages are influenced by Arabic, this likely being where the similarities arise. For example, the word "time" translates to *sa'at* in Tigrinya and *saa* in Kiswahili. Eritreans have a gift for adopting the best qualities of other cultures with which they come into contact. They are exceptionally welcoming to visitors and don't appear to dwell on grudges. Perhaps because theirs is such a unique and strong society, they can confidently embrace foreign things they fancy—like Italian words and foods. Even toward Ethiopians, with whom they had been at war for thirty years, they expressed little open animosity. Of course, it is always easier to wax magnanimous when your side has won.

\* \* \*

In 1996, Eritrea and Ethiopia enjoyed excellent official relations. The top echelon of Ethiopia's current government is largely composed of former rebels from Tigray Province who collaborated with the Eritreans in bringing down the Marxist regime of Haile Mariam Mengistu. One of Ethiopia's main concerns regarding an independent Eritrea was loss of access to the sea. No country aspires to be landlocked, and nearly seventy percent of Ethiopian trade passes through Eritrean ports. But, soon after independence, Eritrea assured Ethiopia of free access to the seaports of Assab and Massawa. Ethiopians I have spoken with, on the other hand, particularly Amharas, have expressed rancor over the matter of Eritrean independence. Nonetheless, I was told by several Eritreans that Eritreans living in and visiting Ethiopia are treated very well, despite any private complaints.

With their neighbor on the western border, the Sudan, relations are not as good. Sudan harbored Eritrean rebels and hundreds of thousands of refugees throughout the war, but ever since Sudan realized that the new Eritrea with its half-Muslim, half-Christian population has no plans to become an Islamic state, relations have soured. Some fundamentalist Muslims in the Sudan view Eritrea as a Christian stronghold on their borders that must be destabilized and conquered. President Isaias Afwerki reported to the United Nations Security Council in 1994 that Sudan supported a *jihad*, an Islamic holy war, into Eritrean territory. Detractors claim, however, that Eritrea uses the Sudan for the "boogie man" syndrome—keeping an enemy without to ensure cohesiveness within.

Supporters of a united Ethiopia and Eritrea emphasize the intertwining history of these two countries. While it is true that strands of Eritrean and Ethiopian early history intermingle, particularly under the highland kingdom of Axum, it generally manifested itself with Ethiopian rulers exercising authority over and making periodic excursions into Eritrean lands to collect slaves and plunder. During all those years, Ethiopians did not migrate to Eritrea in large numbers. In addition, during four hundred years of Turko-Egyptian and then Italian rule, Eritreans maintained intimate contact with Middle Eastern and Mediterranean worlds, while Ethiopia remained largely insular.

That said, it is now commonly held that it was the fifty years of Italian rule that irrevocably separated Eritreans from Ethiopians. Under the Italians, Eritreans made great strides into the twentieth century. A light industrial economy was established, communications improved, roads and railways were constructed, and economic opportunities opened up for a large number of Eritreans. As Eritreans began to develop a collective consciousness of being a people with a connected past and a common destiny, a nationalistic culture was born. It is also worth pointing out that almost all contemporary African states, for better or for worse, are defined by colonial borders rather than their pre-colonial histories. The relatively modern concept of an Eritrean national identity perhaps grew its deepest and most intractable roots during thirty years of Ethiopian subjugation.

Everywhere I turned Asmarinos looked busy. Workmen were installing a new tiled sidewalk in front of the courthouse. Cars and pedestrians navigated mounds of rock and rubble in the streets that were being dug up for new sewers, and buildings were being refurbished. The Italians may have built Asmara but the Eritreans were rebuilding it.

Efficiency, cleanliness, and a penchant for following rules (every Eritrean likes to wag an index finger like a policeman) have led Eritreans to be called the Germans of Africa. Although Asmara is far from being in perfect working order, when a problem arises, so does a solution. This is refreshingly different from the attitude found in other parts of Africa, known as IBM— *inshallah* (God willing), *bokra* (tomorrow), *ma'allesh* (never mind).

I was shocked to learn that Asmara's piped water system was not functioning during my visit. If the pitch of roofs illustrates the amount of rain a country receives, then Eritrea with its pan-flat rooftops gets little to nil. But I experienced none of the effects of a water shortage either at the hotel or in restaurants and the people were the picture of good hygiene. During my first morning shower the water had slowed to a trickle—of course when I was completely lathered in soap—then, miraculously, the water shot out full force. Later, I learned that tankers moved throughout the city, depositing water into large barrels stationed along roadsides and sidewalks.

\* \* \*

"May I look at it?" I asked a boy standing in front of the Housing Bank of Eritrea admiring a glossy brochure. The elfish child handed the booklet to me. It advertised a housing complex being built near the airport by a Korean contractor.

"Very beautiful," the boy said. "Two bedroom apart-a-ment." He flipped the page. "Three bedroom apart-a-ment." The boy beamed with pride, as if he'd designed the Sembel Housing Project himself. The skin on the boy's face had white patches and he wore rumpled clothing. A security guard shooed the two of us away explaining that the German president, Dr. Roman Herzog, was visiting Eritrea for several days as part of a three-country African tour and was heading down Avenue Itegue Taitu, on which we were standing, en route to the old Imperial Palace.

The Germans, as well as the Japanese and Americans, were anxiously knocking on Eritrea's door. And the Germans were making an elaborate show of it: along with Herzog came a retinue of some two hundred people, including journalists. It was rumored that two tons of food and a German chef had been flown in for the occasion. Asmara's government-owned hotels tossed out their less consequential guests, including myself, to make room for this German entourage.

The boy and I moved away from the old Imperial Palace. He told me his name was Haben and asked, "Can you come to my home?" I hesitated, trying first to establish exactly where Haben lived. In Kenya, misunderstandings between locals and foreigners over perceptions of time and distance were commonplace and the subject of much frustration and humor. "It is just there," a Kenyan might say, which could mean anything from a block to several miles away. Haben had to work to convince me that his house was really not far off.

True to his word, we walked only one block to Tegulet Street. We entered one of the many shaded portals in Asmara's alleyways—doorways leading to what I imagined was a simple but charming daily life carried on inside. A sign hung overhead advertising *Autoscuala Jet.* The entrance and stairway leading up to his family's second-floor apartment were surprisingly untidy; I thought of Eritrean households in terms of the few I'd seen in Nairobi, which were immaculate. The hallway was unpainted, trash scattered around, and water from a large storage barrel had splattered on the floor. A *mogogo,* a flying saucer-shaped gas barbecue for cooking *injera,* stood in one corner.

Inside the apartment, Haben's elder brother was bent over mopping the floor with a dirty cloth and murky water. After an initial double take, the diligent brother continued his chores throughout my visit, only occasionally taking a break to stretch his back and interject a few informative sentences into our conversation. Their flat consisted of one large room separated by a curtain. In the first part, where we sat, was a vinyl couch, two chairs, a coffee table, a double bed, a large mirrored armoire, and a sideboard. Newspapers were piled haphazardly on a rack underneath the coffee table. A quaint little balcony overhanging the street was not being used for afternoon tea, as one might like to imagine, but was piled with pairs of shoes.

Haben was in the sixth grade and had just begun studying in English. His English was imperfect, but he spoke with the complete lack of inhibition and gay enthusiasm that only a child could muster. Abel, his brother, spoke English leagues better. Their mother was a nurse and, I was told, was expected to come home soon for lunch. Haben and I browsed through the family photo albums, a common form of entertainment when visiting an African household for the first time. I happened to be carrying in my purse a few photos of my own, and gave one showing snow in Ohio to Haben as a memento of my visit.

In conversation, I mentioned that when my friend Kate arrived from Nairobi we would be going to Massawa.

Haben turned chestnut eyes to meet mine and said, "I want go to Massawa, but my mother say I not go alone. If someone else going...."

I looked over at his brother, still engrossed in his chores, and rolled my eyes. Abel released a wide smile. Like other Eritreans, these boys appeared to have a genteel sense of humor. They responded to sarcasm, which I remember going over like a lead balloon in Kenya where humor is more straightforward and slapstick.

Haben pulled a cooking pot from underneath the sideboard and lifted the dishtowel covering it to show me a saffron-colored paste. *Shiro* he called it, and explained that this orange mash of lentils, chickpeas, and spices was what would be served for lunch. It reminded me of a tale I'd heard about Scotland in the days when people were less affluent. The Scots, the story goes, poured porridge into a drawer, and let it harden. Then, they simply opened the drawer and cut out a few pieces for each meal. Haben and Abel's mother never arrived, so I moved on. I was losing my appetite for lunch anyway. When the mother did come home, I wondered what she would make of the snapshot laying on her coffee table: a towering snow-woman replete with snowball hair and generous breasts that my boyfriend and I had constructed in our front yard in Ohio only a week before.

\* \* \*

Starting at the imposing government offices at one end of town, three boys began to follow me, skipping and dodging around me all the way down Liberation Avenue. Two elderly men waylaid them and held an impromptu discussion, surely admonishing them for pestering visitors. Community child rearing at its best, or as Hillary Clinton's favorite African proverb goes, "It takes a village to raise a child."

I carried on unmolested to Wikianos, a two-story supermarket where foreign housewives and wealthy Asmarinos shop. Wikianos has a wide selection of meats and cheeses in a deli case and generous amounts of imported wine and alcohol at reasonable prices. Upstairs was an assortment of dry goods, including, oddly enough, a rack of men's suit jackets. I was momentarily transported when I heard a short, elderly clerk speaking Kiswahili to an African housewife.

In this temporarily altered world, I blurted out, *"Unazungumza na Kiswahili!"* (You are conversing in Kiswahili!)

*Fabric shop in Asmara*

The woman shook my hand and said, "I don't know where I recognize you from." She spoke to me in a slightly standoffish tone, as if she were a diplomat at a never-ending cocktail party.

Meanwhile, the clerk, an affable man with yellowish-skin and crooked teeth, rattled off his elementary Kiswahili usually reserved for this customer: "*Habari? Mzuri sana? Habari yako? Mzuri?*"(How are you? You are good? How are you? Good?)

I could see through the plate glass window that the three boys who were harassing me earlier had escaped their counselors and were staring at me and laughing. Am I that interesting? The boys tried to be less obvious from that point on. While I was window shopping at a silversmith's, one shop down, they acted as

*The author at the Cathedral in Asmara*

if they were doing the same. Mischievous, young, Eritrea.

As my encounter with Haben had hinted, in Eritrea the simplest action could set off an entire chain of events. I wanted to view the inside of the Catholic Cathedral, a central feature of Asmara, so I wandered up the steps to the arched brick gate. A middle-aged woman in a flowered dress with a white shawl draped over a peach sweater walked up the steps beside me. She had a bluish cross tattooed on her forehead and wore glittery gold sandals. She understood my request and directed a woman in a blue lab coat to unlock the chapel doors. The interior of the chapel was beautiful indeed with marble floors, frescoed ceilings, and azure and gold stained glass windows. I took a few snapshots, and then the woman led me to see the church's tailoring project. In a small shop, a nun sold the end results: lovely embroidered pillowcases, linens, and clothing. Next, the woman led me to her second-floor office so that we could converse. She had a crisp, crackly accent. Even though she spoke English well, I was not confident that she understood me as well as I understood her.

Her name was Amleset. But, she added, it was not the name she had been given at birth. When she was two weeks old, her father left home to fight with the Italians during World War II. Her dad was gone for four years when her mother renamed her Amleset, meaning, "come back." When the father did come back it was only to inform the family that he was leaving again, this time for an Ethiopian woman.

"Those Amhara women...." Amleset said bitterly.

Amleset's jilted mother managed to put all ten of her children through school and was still alive and active at eighty-six years of age. Amleset leaned over a piece of paper. I could see she was counting in her head as she intently listed the number of her mother's progeny.

She looked up and declared, "Seventy. She is very lucky. God blessed her."

A large number of these seventy grandchildren and great grandchildren now live abroad. Amleset's eldest three children live in North America.

Amleset's far-flung family is not unusual in Eritrea. With 750,000 Eritreans in exile from a total population of 3.5 million, this presents the phenomenal scenario that one out of every four Eritreans lives abroad. Calculating that the typical Eritrean family has six members, this means that on average one or two persons per family lives overseas. There is probably not another country in the world with such a high ratio of exiled population. To confirm the large number of Eritreans in America, one can just look at the telephone book. The phone book for the town of Delaware,

Ohio lists frequently called international dialing codes, of which four are African countries, one of these being tiny Eritrea (the others are South Africa, Kenya, and Liberia). This is surely one reason why Eritreans, at least in Asmara, are so welcoming to and interested in foreigners—the foreigner is a link to their relatives abroad.

Amleset guided me by the hand out of the church courtyard. The young woman in the blue smock approached us. She conducted a short, irritable conversation with Amleset.

"She's nipping at me," whispered Amleset.

The church was preparing for a three-day bible teacher conference beginning the next day. Amleset, about the time I had arrived at the Cathedral, had been asked to photocopy something and apparently had not done so. Unshaken, Amleset led me across Liberation Avenue to her favorite snack bar, Cathedral Snack Bar. The owner and Amleset kissed each other on the cheeks four times, as good friends do here, and Amleset ordered two *spris*, a blended fresh fruit drink.

"Your countries have taken care of our children for a very long time," Amleset said, paying for my juice. "So when you people come here we must treat you."

Amleset and I talked about religion and coffee. Eritrea's population is divided nearly evenly between Orthodox Christians and Sunni Muslims. There are also some Catholics, Protestants, and Animists. Little animosity between religions is evident.

We compared the process of making coffee in America—scoop coffee, add water, turn on machine— to the multi-hour ceremony common in this region.

"There is no time in America," Amleset said, and lamented, "It's becoming like that here too."

In Eritrea, as in Ethiopia, making coffee is a time-honored ceremony. No *Mr. Coffee* here. The coffee ceremony is a celebration of friends and family. The preparer—almost always a woman—sits on a low wood stool. She roasts fresh green coffee beans over a charcoal fire using a shallow blackened pan. When the beans are browned, she approaches each of the assembled coffee drinkers and using her hand wafts the aromatic smoke toward their faces. The participants respond by using their own hands to further direct the smoke. The woman returns to her stool and, using mortar and pestle, pounds the roasted beans into grounds which she then funnels into a gourd-shaped clay pot called a *jebena*. Adding water, she sets the *jebena* on hot coals.

The preparer has to watch carefully—when the mixture boils it comes spewing out of the clay pot's narrow, elongated spout. She takes the *jebena* off the coals allowing it to cool momentarily, and then returns it to the fire. Depending on the strength desired, the coffee is re-boiled several times. When the coffee is done, a coarse cloth filter is stuffed into the *jebena's* spout. Finally, steaming coffee is poured into espresso-sized ceramic cups. Popcorn is passed around in a woven basket, while frankincense burns, mingling its rich aroma with the smells of coffee and popcorn. This entire process will be repeated as many as four or more times, until all the guests are satisfied.

Amleset and I finished our juices. We made plans to meet again for coffee at her house. Meanwhile, the young woman in the baby-blue smock must have blown a gasket waiting for that photocopy.

* * *

Generosity is, without doubt, a salient Eritrean trait. A Canadian living in Asmara told me that on occasion the President publicly reminds citizens to be nice to foreigners. But I don't think most Eritreans need to be reminded—it is part of their psyche. For example, I popped into a stationery store near the post office to buy postcards. A calendar on the wall advertised motor oil: "Prima, the Choice of the Free Generation." As I was browsing, an old woman wrapped in a discolored gauzy shawl carried a tray into the store with hot sweat tea in highball glasses. The young clerk handed me one. I saw the young man pay, but he refused to let me pay for mine. I asked him about the old woman.

"She is a beggar," he explained. "I buy tea from her. She goes to the tea shop and brings it here for me."

On another occasion, while I was looking around a bookstore, the owner handed me an artfully photographed postcard of Eritrea.

"How much?" I asked.

"No, it's for you," he insisted.

In a country where, according to 1995 World Bank figures, the GNP per capita is US $100, storekeepers giving away their merchandise to tourists is stupefying.

Another time, I walked into the wide-open front doors of a shop facing the main mosque. A young woman looked up from typing and I asked if she could direct me to the upcountry bus station. She tried to gesture instructions, without success. A stocky elderly man skirted an oversized desk where he had been reading and commanded, "Come with me." We walked around the corner of the building, at which juncture I expected him to point me on my way. Instead, he led me to a beat-up little white car and off we rode together. I commented on the lack of seat belts.

He laughed and said, "Africa!"

In so many words, he told me that his relatives lived in Norway, so he understood the Westerner's obsession with seat belts. The communication went like this:

"Norwegia, family, yes. Like belt."

My meager Italian came in handy in trying to converse. The man told me his daughter's name was Trhaas. Having written two books on African personal names and their meanings, I said, "*fortunata.*" Fortunata is close enough to the expression "brings blessings" that he looked at me surprised, and said, "Yes, yes! Fortunata!"

We zipped over to the country bus station, where he quickly established the daily departure times for buses to Keren and as quickly were back near his office. It was noon, and so many devout Muslims were attending prayer at the mosque that they spilled out into the street like soap bubbles deserting a washing machine. Cloaked in milk white *djellabias* and turbans, the men knelt on reed prayer mats. My impromptu guide maneuvered his miniature car around the prostrate bodies.

"Business typing, computers" he said, describing his business. "France computers, Olivetti."

The man pointed out the family apartment located just above the office. Their modest balcony overlooked the mosque and environs. One section of the balcony wall had a mosaic of a dog made from tiny colored tiles.

These wee bathroom tiles appeared throughout Asmara, covering exterior walls and contouring doorways. Buildings were painted in lively combinations of colors: many the color of sand with a knee-high ocher stripe running along the bottom, with sky blue window frames, shutters, and metal doors. Over open doorways hung strands of sparkling beads, plastic streamers, wooden strips, puffy yarn ropes, and twisted metal links, lending a Bohemian feel to the town. In one restaurant the clock was in the shape of a double heart, in another it was a cutout of a soccer player whose legs swung back and forth with each tick. Between the kitschy clocks, hippie beads, and omnipresent tourism posters, Eritrean interior decorating teeters on a fine line between whimsical and tacky.

\* \* \*

Although it was not marked in English, the gate-keeper assured me I was standing in front of the Ethiopian Embassy.

"See. The flag." He was pointing skyward toward the flag with its green, gold, and red horizontal stripes that have come to symbolize Pan-Africanism.

I had come to apply for a tourist visa to Ethiopia and expected the worst. A British researcher studying food security and conflict in the region, and presently undertaking the task of getting a visa, quelled my fears by saying that the process, although convoluted, was really quite rapid. First, he explained, I must go to Room 6 to pick up a visa application form. Then to Room 7 to have the form verified. I return to Room 6 to pay for the visa and to get a receipt. I go again to Room 7 to show the receipt and to have the visa stamped in my passport. Then I must proceed to Room 5 to obtain an official stamp in addition to the visa stamp. Easy.

By the time I made it to Room 5, I must have been looking hungry. A middle-aged, heavy-set man sat behind a desk watching a videotaped French game show. Learning that I was alone in Eritrea, he suggested we share a meal.

On Saturday night the Ethiopian diplomat and I enjoyed a delicious grilled fish dinner at the Keren Hotel and then set out into Asmara's kind streets, entering the stream of Asmarinos taking their nightly walk, the *giraro*, down Liberation Avenue. A crowd had gathered around a large canvas tent erected in front of the towering Catholic Cathedral. Squeezing through the people, I saw clothes and other consumer goods on display inside the tent and someone turning the handle of a large tumbler. It was a lottery! So many people cued up to try their luck that they overflowed into the street. The police used nightsticks to nudge them gently back into line.

The diplomat and I entered a quiet bar called the Gurgusum. A chic place, it had high ceilings, freshly painted walls, and a kidney-shaped faux-bamboo bar. Like most establishments in this town, wall decorations were wanting, not, I think, because Eritreans are natural minimalists, but more likely because of unavailability of fine art as well as shortages of working capital.

It was the Gurgusum's opening night, and that quaint candle-lit spot rapidly filled to standing-room-only with Asmara's glitterati. The owner, a light-skinned woman who looked like a cross between Sophia Loren and Barbara Streisand, was a buoyant hostess. She greeted each new guest and passed around trays of bite-sized pizzas, pastries, and ham and cheese sandwiches. When we ordered a bottle of Gouder (pronounced like the Dutch cheese *Gouda*), an Ethiopian red wine, the owner hastily dispatched into the street a lanky waiter in black pants and a cardinal red vest over a white dress shirt.

She apologized to us in heavily accented English. "It's opening night," she said, "and I forgot the uh, uh...."

I completed her sentence, "wine opener."

Gouder is a bit harsh and, if you swish it around in your mouth, has a medicinal taste.

Probably setting up an ulterior motive, the diplomat complained of boredom in Eritrea. His wife and children remained in Addis Ababa, he told me, where the schools are better.

"If I had a girlfriend here," he said dreamily, "it wouldn't be so bad. Someone just to go around with."

Ethiopian men are notorious womanizers. Whereas no one would deny that Eritrean men indulge in illicit relations, to me anyway, they didn't act nearly as forward. I asked the diplomat if he found Eritrean women attractive and was surprised to hear him say, "No." He claimed they were weather worn compared with the healthy women of the central highlands of Ethiopia. An Eritrean man later told me a similar thing.

"Ethiopian woman are more voluptuous," the Eritrean had said. "They understand romance. Eritrean women," he continued, "spent so long concentrating on survival, that romance became a lost art."

The last thing I wanted to do on a Saturday night in Asmara was deal with the vaguely romantic pronouncements of a foreign diplomat. I cut the evening short, excusing myself by claiming that I was too tired to stay awake for the midnight opening hour of the city's discos. Meanwhile, I had calculated that our evening's entertainment—full dinner, a bottle of red wine, and mixed drinks—had amounted to only US $12.

The diplomat accompanied me down Liberation Avenue en route to my hotel. I noticed the lottery tent was left unattended, a flap wide open, and the prizes hanging inside. Pedestrians passing by did not even peep sideways to see what was inside. It struck me then just how safe and free of crime Asmara really was. My escort theorized that one reason for this was the homogeneity of the people.

"It's like a village," he said. "Everyone looks out for each other, and looks after visitors." The diplomat expressed great respect, almost reverence, for Eritreans. "An Eritrean would rather eat only one piece of bread each day," he surmised, "than steal or deceive other people." He also admired the physical layout of Asmara, the buildings themselves, and the Eritreans penchant for walking.

Albert Schweitzer, the much-vaunted French physician who devoted most of his life to the West African country of Gabon, once defined a civilized place as one where people don't lie, don't steal, value property, and are kind to animals. Barring perhaps the last factor, I think Schweitzer would have been pleased with modern Eritrea.

The next day at a kitchenware store I asked the clerk, who spoke English perfectly, if it was true that Eritreans love to gamble.

"It's not gambling," she said. "It's the lottery."

I gave her a cockeyed look.

"Well," she confessed and smiled, "I guess that's a form of gambling."

The clerk had such a sweet, familiar disposition that I realized then and there that most of my acquaintances to date had been male. I was starved for female companionship and greatly looked forward to the arrival in Asmara of Kate, a Canadian aid-worker friend from the days when I lived in Kenya.

So merrily absorbed in Asmara's spring-like weather, I wandered around in T-shirts and sandals, and only after several days did I notice everyone else was wrapped up tight in sweaters, jackets, suit coats, and the traditional hand-woven white cotton shawls. Granted it did get cool in the shade, but it was sharply hot in the midday sun. In a traveler's euphoria, I pondered what happened to Eritreans when they were in bad moods. Are they forced to stay inside their homes? Are they politely requested to keep to themselves?

Even in Asmara, however, some days are less than perfect. As Eritrean President Isaias Afwerki himself has said (as recorded by Dan Connell in *Against All Odds*): "You cannot have a society of angels except in heaven." Two cool dudes, probably in their thirties, sat on short metal stools leaning against a wall. The bright sun reflected off their sunglasses as they sipped beers.

"Hello!" one called from across the street. "American?"

I shook my head yes.

"Right on," he growled.

A drunk stumbled out of a bar squinting into the sunlight and mumbled vaguely in my direction, "Hey, babe."

An old grizzled man likewise called out, "Hey, babe," and started walking beside me. He was wearing wrap-around dark sunglasses, a wrinkled brown suit, and had spotty teeth. I was expecting the worst.

"You want a coffee?"

Taken aback by his mildness, I politely replied, "No, thank you."

This same man appeared several hours later at another corner.

"You again!" I said.

"Yes," he said. "I change money and sell old coins."

He showed me a large silver Maria Theresa dollar. I declined the coin, but changed money with him on that corner several times during my trip.

On the next corner, in the post office square, a gangly elderly man clapped and howled with laughter at another slightly loopy old man dancing a jig. As the

dancer moved on, the clapper covered his wrinkled mouth with his hand, his eyes wide open in amusement. The scene reminded me of a line from Ahmadou Kourouma's book *The Suns of Independence*: "When a fool shakes his rattle, it should always be another fool who dances."

# Night
# Out

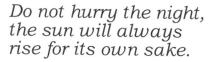

*Do not hurry the night,
the sun will always
rise for its own sake.*

– Eritrean expression

In the first years I lived in Africa, I
fancied myself a budding photographer. My assignments while
working for a development and relief
agency in Kenya included photographing projects for updates and reports to
donor agencies. My brother had been a
professional photographer, so I figured
the skill was somehow genetic. I
invested in a manual camera with a
ponderous zoom lens. After shooting
several rolls of film of the narrow,
enchanting streets of Zanzibar only to
find I had screwed up the light meter,
producing nothing but overexposed
shots, and after spending two days
tooling around Bangkok, Thailand,
taking artistic photos of Thai architecture only to discover that none of them
looked in the least artistic, I came to
the epiphany that not only was I not a
hopeful professional, I was a flat-out lousy
photographer.

So at six o'clock in the evening, as the sun sank beyond the edges of Africa blanketing Eritrea in palace golds and sending its gentle rays across the face of Asmara, I could only admire it.

My placid sunset quickly deteriorated. A group of teenage boys entered the lobby of the Ambassador Hotel, where I had moved upon the German invasion. The boys wore low slung baggy jeans, unwieldy tennis shoes, and *L.A. Gear* jackets. They had come from the direction of the so-called Hard Rock Cafe, a street-level bar adjoining the hotel.

"You fuckin' me up, man," I heard one of them say with an American accent. I shook my head trying to re-establish where I was.

"Just make the call, man," ordered another one.

"Go talk to the white woman," directed a third youth.

A teenager that might have sashayed off the streets of East L.A. sat on a couch beside me.

"Are you boys drinking?" I asked, employing my best parental tone.

"Oh, more than that, man," the boy seated beside me said. "We fucked up." He added, "You like it here?"

"Yes, it's wonderful," I replied.

"Good weather." That was the only positive comment he could muster.

"How old are you?" I asked.

"Fourteen," he replied.

I couldn't keep a lid on my surprise. "Fourteen! You are way too young to be getting 'fucked up.' "

His glassy eyes turned toward me. He pointed to my fringed, tie-dyed skirt and said, "What about Woodstock, man? You're Woodstock."

Okay, he had me there, but I remained taken aback. "Yes, but people at Woodstock weren't fourteen," I retorted. "Maybe they were eighteen or nineteen, perhaps twenty."

With a genuine stroke of sadness breaking into his tone, he countered, "It's when we were born, man." Trying to regain his cool manner, he asked in a low voice, "You ever do c-r-a-c-k?"

"No!" I replied forcefully. "There's no reason to do drugs that strong."

The boy shook his head in agreement, and said, "I like that, man."

A voice called to him from across the room: "Go apologize to the bitch."

"You guys fuckin' me up," returned the boy from the couch. More juvenile delinquents entered the room, shoving each other and cursing.

"Let's get outta here, man," one of them said.

In a menacing cluster, they sauntered onto Liberation Avenue.

I approached the hotel receptionists for insight into what had just taken place. They explained that these youngsters had been sent from America to Asmara for straightening out. Apparently, troublesome European- and American-bred Eritrean children are packed off to the homeland to stay with relatives in hopes that time spent in Asmara, or a village, would instill traditional Eritrean values. These particular cases were proving to be miserable failures.

"Maybe they should be shipped off to the Danakil Desert...or Sawa," I suggested, still somewhat stunned. All Eritreans between the ages of eighteen and forty are required to undergo six months of military training at a place called Sawa, and then spend one year working on nation-building projects. National service teams have constructed dams and wells, repaired roads, terraced hillsides to stop erosion, and planted millions of tree seedlings.

"Yes, yes!" the clerks and other guests agreed.

But those boys are American citizens; they will not be required to do Sawa.

"They don't work, don't go to school," one of the receptionists announced. "They get in trouble with the police."

That was the first time in my life that I had felt deeply ashamed to be American.

"I am embarrassed," I apologized. "My country created this." We all stared out the windows at the boys cavorting in the street. No one blamed me, but everyone assembled agreed it was a shame.

\* \* \*

Samson and Medhani collected me at the Ambassador for another rousing night in Asmara. Betraying their Western sensibilities, they complained vociferously about local drivers.

"These guys are great," I said, trying to mold their views into a wider African context. "You should see how badly people drive in Kenya."

In my estimation, Eritrean drivers mimicked the government policy of moving slowly and cautiously. I recalled that my cabdriver from the airport drove surprisingly conscientiously; he did, however, make one left-hand turn from far inside the oncoming lane with traffic barreling toward us. Samson beat his hand against the horn and guffawed. "I love this," he said. "You can honk your horn here at will—not like Canada."

"Just don't start anything," I warned. "In Egypt they drive with one hand on the wheel, one hand on the horn. It's so annoying."

Samson and Medhani looked at each other and laughed. They said simultaneously, "Like Greece!"

As we raced around a corner, two drunk men sauntered across the street directly in front of the car. I didn't see it, but one of the men slugged Medhani through the open window. Samson slammed on the brakes. He and Medhani, looking like thugs in their heavy black leather jackets, stormed out of the car after the men, yelling, pointing, and accusing. I watched through the rear window, shaking my head in disbelief and mumbling to myself, "boys will be boys." Samson and Medhani summoned into the fray an AK47-toting guard, who happened to be leaning against a wall nearby. The two drunkards were having a hard enough time maintaining their balance, let alone their innocence. They didn't stand a chance against the worldly, wealthy, seemingly superhuman returnees.

"Ah, they'll lock them up for the night," said one of my pals upon returning to the car. "Teach them a lesson."

Returnees, a term frequently heard in Eritrea, is applied to Eritreans who have lived abroad for long periods and have returned to their homeland for resettlement, to establish businesses, or to take protracted vacations as Samson and Medhani had. Returnees tended to be highly educated, skilled, relatively affluent, and cosmopolitan. Eritreans abroad remain staunchly loyal to their motherland and their families. These exiles raised much of the financial support for the thirty-year liberation struggle, and faithfully continue to assist family members back home both monetarily and materially. In fact, remittances from Eritreans abroad accounted for much of the US $139 million in private transfers reported in 1994. Exiles like Samson and Medhani have created a valuable bridge between Eritrean culture and Western culture. For me personally, however, they did more than that—they were good company.

I mentioned, as we drove on, that Eritrea's President Isaias Afwerki was nice-looking. Not since John F. Kennedy, I speculated, has there been a national leader drawing so many favorable comments on his charm and appearance. Samson readily concurred with this observation, while Medhani just shrugged a slightly homophobic "if you say so." More important than Afwerki's looks, Eritreans are quick to point out, their president is a serious and dedicated man.

"The President and those people there," said Samson gesturing toward the imposing colonial-era Government Administrative Center perched on a slight hill. "I can tell you one thing, they are working hard for this country."

The Canadian consultant I talked to earlier in the day reinforced Samson's view of the government.

"It's not propaganda," she qualified, before launching into a series of compliments about the country and its leaders. She spoke of devoted government officials and the absence of bribery, the bane of progress in many other African nations. She explained that to obtain her business license she waited in line and followed the rules just like everyone else. "Not like Italy!" she said.

When the EPLF, the former rebel fighters, started turning their swords into plowshares, they adopted a new name. As of February 1994, they became the People's Front for Democracy and Justice (PFDJ), referred to simply as the Front. This new African government is unusually standoffish about foreign aid. It picks and chooses as it sees fit, declining aid when unacceptable conditions are attached.

"I like to eat," Samson explained while rubbing his stomach, "but not if I can't do things my own way."

Nevertheless, according to the CIA World Factbook, Eritrea's estimated external debt in 1995, two years after independence, was US $162 million. But that was chicken feed compared to neighboring Ethiopia's 4.3 billion dollar debt (1995 estimate) and Kenya's seven billion dollar debt (1992).

"They hear a different drummer," an American banking consultant later told me. "They told the Germans to go packing with their multi-million dollar proposal of experts and equipment."

The classic example of Eritrea's dogged self-sufficiency is the railway reconstruction project. An Italian contractor estimated that it would cost $90 million to refurbish the 73 mile (117 kilometer) narrow-gauge line stretching from Massawa, the major Red Sea port, to Asmara. The government decided to hang onto that lavish sum of money and do the job themselves, for a lot less. Septuagenarians and octogenarians who had worked on the railroad during Italian colonial rule enthusiastically responded to the call to come back to work and proudly toil for their country at an age when most other old men are burrowed deep into retirement.

But, where there is government there will always be critics. Detractors call Eritrea's postwar administration a benevolent dictatorship. They admonish things such as the seemingly impenetrable close-knit group of ex-fighters who run the country, the ineffective system of taxation, the government's dual exchange rate, and unresolved land issues. They note that the government's stubbornness in regard to foreign aid, including unreceptiveness to international aid agencies (NGOs), makes the rural poor suffer needlessly. (Only a few international NGOs remain operational following the introduction of tough restrictions on their activities and a 38% tax on salaries.)

Even those favorably disposed would have to admit that the government is controlling. "Social engineering" is a term that comes to my mind when examining the current Eritrean government. The president himself, during a trip to the United States, referred to his method of rule as "controlled democracy."

I had visited the Government Administration Center earlier that day to inquire whether a group of foreigners could purchase a private vacation residence in Eritrea. (With land issues unclear and property price quotes ranging wildly from US $50,000 to US $500,000, our chances didn't look good.) Upon entering the Center, I was confronted by a long row of receptionists sitting behind bank teller-style wooden counters. All the receptionists were men and, judging from their wooly hairdos and green jackets, were recently demobilized freedom fighters. Each sat below a sign indicating a different ministry or office. I bent down to speak through the cutaway part of the glass. One of these battle-hardened men pulled up a chair and instructed me to come behind the counter and sit next to him while he explained his government's policies.

"The government is taking services to the people," he began, "so that people do not crowd the cities." Stemming urban migration seemed admirable; overcrowded cities are a source of grave problems in other African countries. "Our government is rebuilding," he continued. "The roads are too narrow, and they make them wider."

The clerk did not talk about rumors that the government was trying to discourage Asmara's seedy back-street bars, products of the days of Ethiopian occupation, in favor of more wholesome entertainment. And he wouldn't have dared broach the subject of the conspicuous absence of beggars on Asmara's streets. According to several foreign newspaper accounts, indigents are rounded up by the police and carted to an old tuberculosis hospital in Asmara or assigned to public works projects. Word on the street claimed that beggars are sent to camps where they grow their own food and are expected to become self-sufficient. At any rate, Asmara's citizens seem to be in sync with the government on this issue. Beggars who slip through the cracks and hit the streets of Asmara, young and old alike, are promptly scolded by locals eager to ensure that visitors have a hassle-free experience.

"Beggars dress nicely now," Samson speculated, "so that they won't be spotted and sent away."

Although they lurk like caged demons in the backyard, most Eritreans have managed to put such criticisms aside for the time being. Of the Eritreans I met, support for their government was not only universal, it was enthusiastic. If it is true that a country exists because its people consent to being governed, then there is probably no place on Earth more qualified than Eritrea to call itself a nation. In 1994, the National Assembly formed a fifty-member National Constitution Commission to hammer out a constitution. The constitution would create a parliamentary system with a strong chief executive, and, according to the U.S. State Department Country Report on Human Rights Practices for 1997, promises to establish democratic freedoms and an independent, although weak, judiciary.

Presidential and parliamentary elections are scheduled for 1997. (As of August 1998, elections had yet to be held and the final draft of the constitution was not yet released.) Observers say the Eritreans have a history of democratic traditions. John C. Rude, in an article in the March-April 1996 edition of *The Humanist,* claims that these traditions are "only matched by the Swiss." If the voter turnout is anything like that of the independence referendum, in which an astounding ninety-eight percent of eligible voters participated, and the election is free and fair (there is no reason to think it would be otherwise), Eritrea could set an example of democratic participation not just for Africa, but for the whole world.

Swinging their creaking rental car through Asmara's back streets, Samson and Medhani finally located a *mes* house in a darkened neighborhood. To my surprise—considering I found Eritrea the safest country in the world—Samson locked the car, saying, "I don't trust this area." We entered the bleak front room of a private home. The concrete walls had been painted with super high-gloss paint, the bottom half eggshell white, and the top half teal. Chairs and tables were aligned against the walls in a square formation, allowing patrons to observe one another in an unflattering light. Except for the mother and daughter whom lived and worked there, no one was in the *mes* house. With sleepy eyes, they were preparing to close up for the night and sink back into their private domain when we came in.

Any business is good business, so the girl brought to our table a bottle of *mes,* a mixture of honey, water, and *gesho* (woody hops) poured into used liquor bottles, sealed with wax, and allowed to ferment for eight days. With a masterful flick of her wrist, the daughter popped the wax seal off the bottle onto the floor. She poured the cloudy amber liquid into our drinking vessels—bottles with bulbous bottoms and long narrow necks, like something resident in a science lab. The girl repeatedly walked over and refilled our beakers as we drank and chatted.

We talked about a story Samson heard when he was a child concerning an unusual Afar custom. The Afars, who make up only four percent of the Eritrean population, are seminomadic herdsmen with a fierce reputation. A Muslim people of Hamitic stock closely related to Oromos and Somalis, the Afars inhabit Denkalia, one of the world's most forbidding locales. Within northern Denkalia lies part of the Danakil Depression, a basin dipping down to 380 feet (116 meters) below sea level, making it among the hottest spots on earth; temperatures there can climb to 122 degrees Fahrenheit (50 degrees Celsius). Running along the Red Sea coast south of Massawa, Denkalia was one of the last regions in Africa to be explored by Europeans. Certainly the Europeans were put off by 1881 and 1884 reports of Italian explorers who were murdered by the Afars. Not until 1928 did the first European successfully cross Denkalia.

The particular Afar custom in question requires a man to present his bride-to-be with a set of male genitalia as a sign of courage symbolizing that he has killed a man in battle. The following is a grossly simplified version of Samson's story, but it leads to an interesting point. One day a father and his son were walking in the countryside. An Afar tribesman approached them demanding a set of testicles. The father told the Afar to take his son's testicles, not his own. Upon hearing this, Samson recalled, adults would become enraged. The father already had his children, they would protest, and yet he denied his son the same opportunity. Such an angry reaction reflects a salient Eritrean, and indeed African, trait: an intense love of children. Eritrean families with eight or even twelve children are not uncommon. Samson and Medhani said that during Ethiopian rule, when a 6:30 p.m. curfew was imposed, birth rates rose dramatically. Of course, the protracted war claimed the lives of scores of those children—some 200,000 according to one source.

"What is life," Samson said one of his relatives had asked, "but to watch your children grow?"

Between sips of *mes*, Medhani spoke of leaving Holland, where he works with machinery and computers and, like many Eritreans, dreams of moving to Addis Ababa to establish his own business.

"I have a plan," he said obliquely but confidently. Despite an irrefutable love for their homeland, both Samson and Medhani told me they prefer Addis Ababa, the capital city of Ethiopia, to Asmara. Addis Ababa, I would discover, had something of a boomtown feel and there was an active nightlife. Like many of Asmara's Western residents, my friends complained of nothing to do in Asmara, simply not enough diversion. Conversely, this was exactly what I found so appealing about Asmara as a destination: never feeling as though you're missing anything. There are no world-class theaters, no chic nightclubs, no compulsions to visit this or that celebrated church, museum, or historic sight. Time was plentiful to soak up atmosphere and to concentrate one's energies on the architectural variety and ample human interactions—like spending an evening drinking home-brewed wine with two new acquaintances in a deserted *mes* house.

Shortage of entertainment aside, one factor preventing Eritreans abroad from moving back home—particularly those from industrialized nations—is the rate at which the government is liberalizing politics and economics. Many consider it sluggish. Almost certainly the national service program is another element inhibiting exiles from returning.

"People can't come back," speculated Samson, "because they don't want to do national service."

Like many Eritrean policies, on the surface Sawa and national service appear sound; it is the finer points of implementation that are subject to scrutiny. The current upper-age requirement of forty years is rather high, and if fully implemented could create economic havoc for families certainly and perhaps for the country too. To date, however, mostly young people—about 15,000 per round—have been conscripted. On an upcoming bus trip to Massawa, I would see camps along the roadside that looked far from inviting, with tents erected atop rocky outcrops under a blazing sun. But those who fought for the country's freedom suffered worse conditions and came out, many say, a better people. At any rate, national service might just

*The author at a mes house with Samson and Medhani*

be the essential ingredient in rebuilding a nation ravaged by war, a country that has little working capital, and that doesn't want to fall into the trap of dependency on foreign aid.

The old mama at the *mes* house stopped under the weight of a yellow blanket wrapped around her head. She must have been wishing we would finish already. At 10 p.m. we were out late for this sleepy part of the city. Apparently, the *mes* houses were busiest immediately after work.

"This was where our fathers spent all their time," said Samson kidding with Medhani.

A drunken straggler took advantage of the still open door and slipped into a seat against the opposite wall. With utterly glazed eyes, he asked me to take his photograph, but I didn't want to waste the film. We paid the patient ladies the three *birr* we owed—less than fifty cents—and left them alone to contend with their latest arrival.

# Keren

*The time when everyone
in this country will
feel relieved will be
when we are not asking
anyone to give us help.*

— President Isaias Afwerki

There are few must-see, must-do sights in Eritrea, but Asmara's one should-see can't-miss sight is the imposing brick Catholic Cathedral on Liberation Avenue. Built in 1922, the cathedral was designed in Lombard style by Scanavini, an Italian architect. Another Asmara venue is the former Imperial Palace, known locally as the *Ghibi*, an impressive buttery yellow and cream building that now houses the National Museum. Ferdinando Martini, the first Italian civil administrator, built the *Ghibi* in 1897 in neo-classical style. The central market, the *idaga*, is a lively and colorful spot located north of the Catholic Cathedral. The Mai Jahjah fountain (pronounced mah-ee-JAH-jah) isn't necessarily awe-inspiring, but worth the visit if only to learn to say and repeat its whimsical name as often as possible. "I visited Mai Jahjah today....You know, when I walked past the Mai Jahjah this morning...."

Beyond Asmara, travelers might go to Keren for silver shopping and provincial atmosphere and to Massawa or Assab for port life and the sea. Other than that, one finds a few odd ancient Axumite ruins, some reminders of World War II, and, I was told, interesting sights from the war of liberation. Eritrea does not exactly overwhelm a visitor with compelling destinations, and that is one of its finest features. The country isn't so much a place to explore, as to experience. No rushing around, no pressure, just absorb.

I shoved a few essentials into a backpack and headed for the bus to Keren. The altitude in Eritrea is so much higher than at home that just repacking my suitcase had taken my breath away. Keren is only 65 miles (105 kilometers) northwest of Asmara, but the bus journey takes about three hours due to the slow, twisting descent through rugged mountains. Backpacking felt unusual, as I had never really done it before, with the exception of a rather cushy, by comparison, three-month post-college train trip through Western Europe. But there I was, fifteen years later, in Maine Woods sandals, a canvas pack slung over my shoulders, traipsing through the bustling streets of Asmara to the country bus station.

Passengers waved me into a seat beside a colorfully dressed Bilen woman. I sat down, not realizing that the woman's young son was vying for the same seat. Apparently children's passage is free on upcountry buses, but they are expected to share a seat with their guardians. The bus hadn't chugged far down the road before it was full of bobbing heads. Eritreans, and Ethiopians, I later learned, have an incredible capacity to sleep sitting upright, even under the most jarring or treacherous of conditions. The Bilen boy, teetering on the corner of our padded bench seat, finally managed to get comfortable and fell asleep with his head in the crook of my arm. His mother protested in her language that it would hurt me, but I signaled

*My Seatmate on the bus to Keren*

"no problem." I cupped the boy's hot forehead in my palm. His soft wavy black hair rubbed against my arm, while smells of earth and sweat mingled in the constricted air of the bus.

"I saw you at the Ethiopian Airlines office," I said to the a British man seated behind me.

This initiated non-stop conversation. James, with spiky hair, eyeglasses, and earrings, was one of ninety or so volunteers working in Eritrea through the Peace Corps and the British equivalent, the VSO. James did the lion's share of the talking, answering all my queries about the country's inner workings. He asked very little about me and talked even less about himself. This is a trait I remember adopting in Kenya. After living abroad so long, you begin to tire of striking up relationships with the streams of people who pass through the country and through your life. You learn to provide information to help a voyager along, to chat openly, but to give sparingly of yourself.

In our three-hour bus ride, James managed to temporarily shatter all my positive images of Eritrea.

He didn't like Tigrinya music or the language, calling it harsh in comparison with Amharic.

"Eritreans," I said venturing a positive statement, "are supposed to be less arrogant than Ethiopians."

"The Eritreans spread that rumor," he retorted.

John Gunther, in his epic book from the 1950s *Inside Africa*, commented that Eritreans were "milder people than Ethiopians...more advanced in some respects, and not so haughty." James said Eritreans were, in fact, conceited and aggravatingly sexist. He lamented the fact that he couldn't be friends with local women at his volunteer site. Furthermore, he felt it was difficult to befriend any Eritreans beyond a superficial level. I wondered if that wasn't partially a function of language barriers. He acknowledged that could play a part.

According to James, the Ministry of Finance released a statement claiming that Eritrea would be like Singapore in ten years.

"It's misleading and deceitful," he said. "Maybe in one hundred years, but now a large percentage of the population is illiterate. It is not one city, like Hong Kong, to consider, but a whole country."

Eritrea does have overwhelming factors working against it: eighty percent of the country's population make a living by subsistence agriculture or pastoralism; the GNP per capita, using World Bank figures for 1995, is just US$100; and the life expectancy rate at birth, according to UN figures for 1990-95, is a mere 50.4 years.

Only twenty percent of adult males and ten percent of adult females can read and write. Incredibly, the primary source of foreign exchange is an estimated US $75 million per year, sent to the country by its citizens living abroad. In 1995, according to the *CIA World Factbook*, Eritrea imported an estimated US$ 404 million worth of goods and exported only US $81 million, meaning a US $323 million trade deficit. A Ugandan colleague once told me that while working in Eritrea he had driven all over the country, and he found Eritreans to be the poorest people on earth.

On the plus side, at independence in 1993 Eritrea was in the enviable position of having no external deficit because Ethiopia agreed to assume all foreign debt. Because of its position along one of the busiest shipping lanes in the world, Eritrea has generations of experience with international trade and entrepreneurship, as well as a history of intermingling cultures. Eritrea also can claim many skilled workers; at the onset of Ethiopian rule in 1952, Eritrea held one-third of the industrial capacity of the federation. In the mid-1990s, closed industries are reopening and new ones are springing up. Manufactured products include textiles, leather goods, processed foods, chemicals, glass, construction materials, and matches. Considerable mineral wealth and investment potential also exist. In 1995, investors pledged US $250 million to the country. For example, Anadarko Petroleum Company signed a deal with the Eritrean Ministry of Energy, Mines and Water Resources to begin exploration for oil and gas in the Red Sea, and Ashanti Goldfields of Ghana secured a three-year license to explore for gold. Sheraton Hotels and Coca-Cola had projects planned for the country. Also in 1995, Eritrea received US $20 million in aid from America, making it the biggest per capita recipient of U.S. aid in Africa.

Unlike James, many onlookers painted a bright future for Eritrea. Some have suggested that the country could become a gateway to the region, something resembling Lebanon in its heyday. Eritrea is an attractive land, with a diverse and tolerant populace where Islam and Christianity coexist peacefully. In particular, Eritrea has close economic, cultural, and historical ties with Ethiopia giving it access to the potentially huge Ethiopian market of nearly sixty million people.

James remarked that Eritrea's lowlanders, amongst whom he works, are much nicer than the highlanders, referring largely to the people of Asmara, and theorized that this might hold true everywhere in the world. That is equivalent to saying that people in the highlands of Kenya aren't as nice as coastal Kenyans. Or, perhaps, that coastal Californians are nicer than those living in Sierra Nevada, which I found difficult to fathom.

I uttered, "Well, at least the bus drivers seem careful."

He told me that buses were, in fact, known to careen over the steep edges of the escarpment. Thank you, James....

The road to Keren winds through mountains in a continual series of hairpin turns. It really is a brilliant road, an amazing feet of engineering by the Italians. The corners are braced by fine stone walls that, from a distance, resemble medieval fortresses. But the curves are not very wide, and although drivers move with exceeding caution, it was still a nail-biting experience to meet up with other vehicles.

In this region, the landscape is so stark and barren of vegetation that it leaves only the colors of burlap, reed, and raffia to undulate into the horizon. Dry river beds, reminiscent of northern Kenya's *laggas*, cut through the valleys. An occasional papaya oasis broke the grip of dryness, while goats munched on what vegetation remained.

"They should shoot them all," said an ever-cheerful James, "they do so much damage."

Elder residents of Eritrea often recall the olden days when thick forests covered the hills surrounding Asmara. Several described them as "very dangerous" referring to the wild animals—elephants, lion, and leopard—that used to live under the canopy of green. The barren land passing by the bus window made that hard to imagine. Less than one hundred years ago, thirty percent of the country was covered by forest, today, according to a World Bank press release, the figure is closer to twelve percent. Ethiopian soldiers cut down trees for fuelwood and to deny cover to Eritrean liberation fighters. Eritreans also cut the trees for fuel and for housing. A devastating drought in northeast Africa in the 1980s added to the orgy of deforestation. To make matters worse, during their retreat in 1991, Ethiopian soldiers implemented a "scorched earth" policy uprooting virtually all the remaining trees in their path. These factors combined to create serious soil erosion problems, which in turn had a negative impact on agricultural production. In the mid-1990s, about one-third of the country's population was dependent on food aid for either part or all of their yearly food supply.

I noticed extensive terracing along hillsides, even in locations far from human settlement. James explained that the terracing had been done under the auspices of food-for-work programs. Closer to Asmara, where the air was lighter and cooler, there were many eucalyptus trees growing on the terraces. According to James, during school holidays, children are required to take part in *ma'etot*, a development program that includes planting trees throughout the country. Over twenty million tree seedlings had been planted so far. During the war, eucalyptus was the tree of choice, because it grows quickly and provides good fuelwood and housing materials. Unfortunately, eucalyptus trees also absorb large quantities of groundwater and use so much of the nutrients from the soil that indigenous species—where they exist—are often blotted out.

\*    \*    \*

On a large piece of canvas a painting of a man, a woman, and a snake had been strung up in the main square of Keren town. As I stood wondering what the Tigrinyan writing said a tall, slovenly man with acne and cloudy eyes happened by. The man explained that the painting advertised a movie called *Blood by Blood*. Roughly, he said with a fixed grimace, it was a love story: its moral, that fighting is not the solution to one's problems. A returnee from Germany and France, Kesete offered to buy me a coffee. Initially I hedged because his manner was so uncommonly coarse and his English faltering, but I was there for the experience.

We climbed a few steps to one of the teashops over-looking the town's main roundabout. The teashop was astonishingly basic compared with its grand street appearance. Low stools, some made from woven colored plastic and others from twine, were scattered haphazardly across a concrete floor. The tables were rickety and painted that ubiquitous sky blue. A young girl brought over a gourd-shaped aluminum coffee pot with a wad of plastic strips jammed into the neck to serve as the strainer. She set the pot on a small metal tray that already held two espresso-sized cups and an embossed aluminum sugar bowl. The ginger they add to the coffee in this region left a biting feeling at the back of my throat. Kesete spooned mounds of sugar into his tiny cup, then added coffee, and stirred. I thought to myself: "A little coffee with your sugar."

"I love sugar," he said to me, reading my mind.

Across the room sat a gaunt old man in a grimy white gown. His white turban was so loosely tied it looked as if someone's laundry accidentally landed on his head. The entire time we sipped our coffee the man stared at me with old dog eyes and a pleasant expres-sion. No one in the shop appeared fazed by the *ferenji* (white foreigner), really. Kesete called himself a trans-lator and boasted that he was fluent in ten languages, listing them all several times. He was in Keren spend-ing some "free time" before starting a job with a German aid agency.

"Asmara is too cold, Massawa too hot," he said jus-tifying the choice of Keren for spending his free time.

"Oh," I blurted out. "I need to get some of these coffee cups!"

Next thing I knew, Kesete was dragging me through the market in search of those particular coffee cups made from gold-colored glass. A group of women stopped and pointed at me.

"They recognize you from the bus," Kesete said.

After several inquiries we found the right shop. It was crowded with visiting old men. Never in my life have I heard so much animated discussion over the purchase of such a trivial item. Finally, the owner

*Keren Town*

dragged over a ladder to retrieve the cups wrapped in styrofoam and stored high up on a shelf. The assembled old men chuckled repeatedly during the transaction, but Kesete remained annoyed and grim throughout.

Keren, the Italian-built capital of Senhit Province (now Anseba), has a population of around 60,000. More than the European-style city of Asmara, this town is reminiscent of the Africa I remembered from project site visits to rural areas of East Africa. Keren's children, covered in a matte of dust, crowded around me and stared. They had snotty noses and ear to ear smiles. All of them wanted to shake my hand and to squeeze into a photograph. They were much easier to shake off, however, than children I'd encountered elsewhere. When you waved goodbye to Keren children, the gesture was understood.

I meandered down a dirt road on the outskirts of town, passing alongside traditional mud-and-thatch homes. A toddler snuck up behind me and grabbed my shirt. Admittedly I was surprised, but I wheeled around and let out a wildly exaggerated scream. The girl's eyes widened to nearly the size of her face as she turned and raced down the lane yelping. I waited until she caught up with her little companion and then ran after them. Tiny screams erupted, to the wholehearted delight of several young men who were walking past and had witnessed the scene.

\* \* \*

The Keren Hotel, were I decided to stay, held a commanding position on a slight hill at the center of town. Like its sister hotel in Asmara, it was a token of former days of colonial glory. The hotel's window and doorframes were hewn of walnut, or some similarly rich hardwood. The door handles were Art Deco era, and the stairs were made of white marble, Italian no doubt. The spacious bedrooms had high ceilings. But the mattresses sagged so badly that they must have been purchased in the 1930s along with the door handles.

I looked forward to a peaceful meal in the hotel's cavernous dining room. The waitress brought the usual mixed salad of lettuce, tiny tomatoes, and onions, swimming in copious oil and vinegar. This was followed by spaghetti carbonara, hot fresh bread, and papaya juice to die for. As I was finishing the meal, a petite British woman with short-blond hair, wearing an impressive selection of silver jewelry that blared "world traveler," entered the room. Being the only two people in sight, we nodded friendly hellos and simultaneously said, "join me" and "may I join you."

Rachel worked as an accountant on films, but she hoped to establish herself as a professional photographer. To expand her portfolio, she visited Ethiopia, where—along with hoards of other journalists—she photographed the elaborate Timket, Ethiopian Orthodox epiphany, ceremonies. In Eritrea, she was photographing railway reconstruction work on behalf of a friend who planned to make a documentary of the railway project as a symbol of Eritrea's commitment to rebuilding their country largely by themselves. After an enjoyable conversation, both of us bowed out for an early night's sleep.

Wedding season was upon Eritrea, but neither Rachel nor I knew it. Farmers had just finished harvesting, leaving plenty of time and food for celebrations. For Christians, elaborate festivities had to be squeezed in before the fast-approaching Lenten season, a period marked by fasting and austerity. Eritreans have an open wedding policy; anyone who hears the ruckus is welcome to attend. I learned about this custom earlier in Asmara. When declining a dinner invitation, I had used the excuse that I was invited to a wedding (I had been invited, but was not planning to attend). This was not a clever tactic.

"We can go!" the gentleman exclaimed happily.

I replied, "No, you see, it is the sister of someone whom I barely know; I have never even met the bride."

My admirer remained upbeat: "It doesn't matter here! Anyone can go to an Eritrean wedding!"

One of these free-for-alls happened to be taking place on the rooftop of the Keren Hotel. When Rachel and I retired to our respective rooms at 8:30 p.m. the receptionist informed us that the wedding would only carry on a few more minutes. A monotonous pounding beat reverberated through the high ceiling of my room. Bah-boom. Bah-boom. Bah-boom. After about an hour of listening to it, I began to suspect I had made a serious mistake in choosing the Keren Hotel, despite its remnants of grandeur.

By 10:30 p.m. the pounding music not only showed no signs of abating, it had grown several decibels louder. For awhile my Walkman and headphones provided refuge from the racket, but just as I reached the verge of sleep, the batteries died. Bah-boom...bah-boom...bah-boom. It echoed through the walls. Bah-boom...bah-boom...bah-boom. It sounded as if some colossal space alien had landed on top of the Keren Hotel, its dastardly heartbeat pulsing as it pondered how to go about devouring Keren town.

I tramped over to Rachel's room in my red and white pinstriped cotton pajamas.

"Are you sleeping?" I asked through the door.

"Are you kidding?" she growled.

Rachel's ire was raised; she had specifically and pointedly requested a quiet room because she had been feeling ill and desperately needed a good night's sleep. The receptionist had assigned her one of the hotel's quietest rooms, but had neglected to inform her that a wedding would be staged on the roof. I pulled a cardigan over my pajamas, shoved on my glasses, and we stomped out into the night to look for another hotel. As luck would have it, a bus from the lowlands had pulled into town that evening, meaning that every hotel in Keren was packed full. The Siciliano was so crowded that the front veranda, lined with cots of dead-to-the-world bodies, looked like an open-air army hospital.

While walking with the receptionist from the Siciliano to two other hotels, both full, we could hear the wedding music wafting through the dark streets. We could see the colored lights twinkling and the gala taking place on the rooftop patio of the four-story Keren Hotel. There was really no escaping it. Resigned to our fate, Rachel and I returned to our hotel rather refreshed after strolling through the dusty streets in the warm night air. To our pleasant surprise, the guests, all bundled up in their white gauzy clothing were finally leaving en masse. Of course, disassembling a wedding doesn't happen in a snap of the fingers, so it was a good hour later before the hotel became quiet. At that juncture I realized, to my horror, that another wedding was transpiring in the town somewhere. It was more distant, but nonetheless, the bah-boom...bah-boom...bah-boom carried on into the wee hours of the morning. At last, I fell into a deep, delirious sleep.

I heard the door swing open and the sound of feet dragging across carpet. Even in a sleepy haze, I knew all too well that the floor of my hotel room was bare marble, not carpeted, but I decided to open my eyes anyway. There, at the foot of the bed, suspended a few feet above the ground, a body wearing a hunter green camouflage shirt and dark pants floated in thin air. There was no head; one arm waved up and down. I was overcome by that sinking feeling one gets when frightened out of one's wits in a dream but unable to

*The livestock market outside of Keren town
during a lull in the hubub*

scream. After a brief struggle with my vocal chords, I managed to coax out a weak, "Get out! Get out!" I added a crackling, "Ahhh!" The apparition vanished.

I worried that I might have woken up other guests with my wobbly scream, but the hotel was silent. Then I became concerned about my sanity. I had to take some safety precautions: Let's see, which part of one's body does a headless camouflage-wearing ghost attack? I pulled the covers tightly across my chin to protect my neck. For what felt like hours I lay stiffly on the bed glancing around the room, wide-eyed, like a searchlight at sea.

When the sun shone into my room in the morning, I took note of the green faux-marble walls; they looked suspiciously similar to the colors in the ghost's shirt. Nevertheless, I fully intended to check out of Room 6 of the Keren Hotel.

Comrades after a long frustrating night, Rachel and I set off together to investigate the outskirts of Keren town. The first site we encountered was a World War II cemetery...hmm. Hundreds of corpses of soldiers, Italian and Eritrean, lay under uniform rows of chalk-white grave markers. Vibrant bougainvillaea, Italian

*Young friends come easily in Keren*

flags, and modest shrines broke the blinding white-
ness. The graveyard was well-tended and held sublime
views of Keren town, the sight of major battles in 1941
between the British and Mussolini's forces. The majority of the headstones read simply IGNOTO, unknown.
An ideal breeding ground for ghosts, I'd say.

Further along the road leading south from town,
we found the Monday livestock market unfolding in a
walled compound on a hillside. Men and boys had
gathered to examine, discuss, and test-drive animals.
Cattle, sheep, and goats were bought and sold in the
upper half of the corral, while in the lower part, camels
and donkeys were on display. The two sections were
separated by a high wall and joined by a set of stairs.

Whether she possessed a photographer's skills I
didn't know, but Rachel certainly displayed a photographer's spunk. She effortlessly approached Muslim
herdsmen and requested to take their photographs.
These men—tall, lean, somber, and elegant in long
white robes and turbans—broke into warm smiles for
Rachel, gladly posing beside their camels.

Meanwhile, I and some tagalongs, two girls about
seven-years-old who had latched on to us earlier while
walking through their neighborhood, squinted into the
sun listening to a teenage boy mounted on a donkey
rattling away at me in schoolhouse English.

*One of our girlguides posing inside a chapel built
into a tree trunk, near Keren*

"Mine is a low life," he said. "I want to live in
America. America is classical life."

I protested and argued that Eritrea was a good
country.

"I know my life one hundred percent," he lectured.
"You don't know my life. I have to walk up and down
hills to get food. Mine is a low life."

I was on the verge of reminding this adoles-
cent that his people had given their lifeblood for
thirty years to make Eritrea a country he could be
proud of, when my speech was interrupted. As if
a flash flood had struck, a spooked herd of cattle
poured through the wide stairway, bulls with
horns bent downward charging into the crowd.
The market erupted into panic. Buyers and
sellers made a dash for walls and exits. Men
pulled me behind them, toward them, around
them and next thing I knew I was flung out the
entranceway. I stood breathlessly with my back
against the gate. Rachel and our two tiny friends
were still inside. After things calmed down, I went
back in to identify their trampled remains.

One of our little girlfriends looked up at me with a shocked expression and beat her hand against her heart to show me that she had been afraid. I nodded in agreement.

"It is not just you," an English-speaking bystander explained, "We are all afraid. I never see this."

Still milling in the bottom enclosure, the bulls started kicking up dust again and charging people and other animals. This time, Rachel and I were the first to shimmy up the perimeter wall and others followed suit. Everyone sat patiently, alternating laughter with chatter and signs of worry. A herder eventually materialized who appeared to be in control of the rogue animals. He indicated that the path was clear and walked us in a wide arc around the compound and out the gate.

Despite the fact that sleepy Keren town just kept serving up one course of excitement after another, Rachel and I were anxious to leave. We didn't want to risk any more weddings, apparitions, or raging bulls. At the bus depot we found approximately two bus-loads-worth of passengers standing in an orderly cue under the blazing sun waiting for the next coach to Asmara. An Orthodox Christian festival was taking place in Massawa that week, so in addition to the usual traffic, crowds were trying to make their way southeast through Asmara to the coast. Waiting in that line was clearly not going to get us back as quickly as we would have liked to the steamy showers and peace of mind that Asmara afforded. We decided to hitchhike. As we were walking from the hotel, I realized I had never actually hitched a ride before. A few yards past the town center, I asked Rachel if we weren't supposed to stop and try to get a lift.

Rachel scoffed: "You have to walk out of town."

On the edge of Keren town, where boxy houses painted the citrus fruit colors of Miami Beach clung onto hillsides, we discovered that we weren't the only people with the bright idea to hitchhike. Several Eritreans sat beside their overnight bags in the shade of trees at a spot where vehicles must slow down.

Luckily, one of them, a preacher, took an immediate liking to us. He flagged down a minivan for himself and inquired if they could squeeze in two *ferenji*. The driver recognized the preacher and agreed under the stipulation that if the van was pulled over for over-crowding, the strangers paid the fine.

"Of course we will," Rachel and I agreed with visions of hot tap water and cappuccinos dancing in our heads. "Just get us to Asmara!"

Chatting with our preacher friend, Rachel and I sat contentedly on the metal wheel arch. From that particular low-down vantagepoint, it looked as if the vehicle teetered on the brink of sheer cliffs. Several men offered their seats, but we declined, content and grateful just for the ride. The faces filling the minivan were extraordinary. A young man in the back seat was the spitting image, in a richer hue, of Michelangelo's *David*. Whereas in Asmara I might put the majority of noses into the button category, out here they looked larger, more hook-like. The Italians may have left a beautiful capital city, the skill for crafting nice shoes, a thirst for cappuccino, and craving for pasta and gelato, but those conquering Turks and Egyptians bequeathed their noses.

# Massawa

*The incorruptibility and dedication of these people is extraordinary.*

— Robert Houdek,
   former U.S. Ambassador
   to Eritrea

A compact four-wheel drive vehicle pulled up beside me as I was walking back to the Ambassador Hotel. The two men inside offered me a ride.

"It's very close," I said in refusal.

"But we are riding," they retorted, "and you are walking and you are the visitor."

Guileless generosity is hard to decline. I took the ride. Asmerom and Tirfe were both visiting Eritrea from Saudi Arabia, their adopted home where they had been working in hospitals for over a dozen years. Two blocks later, back at the Ambassador Hotel, they treated me to a fresh juice at the Hard Rock Cafe.

Finally burned out on people after making dozens of new acquaintances in a short span of time, I resisted Asmerom and Tirfe's friendship and their requests to meet later for drinks or dinner. Their insistence that they drive me to the airport to collect Kate started to grate on my nerves.

"Look," I said honestly, "I am really sorry we didn't meet earlier because now there are so many people with whom I have made plans, that I don't really have time to do anything more."

They caught my drift.

"We are just picnicking," said Asmerom, who spoke English more fluently than his companion. "We'll take you to the airport, and it doesn't mean you have to spend time with us."

At the airport Asmerom, Tirfe, and I stood under the glaring midday sun interminably waiting for Kate. We watched passengers exiting the terminal and greeting their families. They embraced waiting relatives as if holding on for dear life itself. It was impossible to distinguish tears of joy from tears of grief: likely there were elements of both. The mixed emotions can partly be explained by an Internet message from Hidaat, an Eritrean exile (found in "The Birth of a Nation in Cyberspace," *The Humanist*, March-April 1996). Writing about an impending visit to Asmara, Hidaat explained that her mother died only months before Eritrea became free. Hidaat's message read:

> She won't be ululating at the airport like other mothers. What words can describe the void and sadness that is steady in my heart as I kiss a cold stone that has become her home now...I have only four weeks in Eritrea to balance a lifetime of chaos and somehow find some new perspective for the future.

The two generous men, toward whom I was not feeling very affable, spent more than two hours with me waiting for Kate's arrival. They drove us back to our hotel, and finally, as promised, set us free.

Kate and I dined that evening at the Asmara Restaurant beside the post office. This unassuming spot had quickly become my favorite for indulging in local fare, referred to in both Eritrea and Ethiopia as "national food." On one wall of the Asmara hung the ever-popular poster of Eritrean rebel fighters, looking very seventies with fuzzy Afros and brief khaki shorts, climbing atop a hill to plant the Eritrean flag. An oversized poster of a sculptured English garden entirely covered another wall like wallpaper.

Eritrean and Ethiopian cuisine uses neither sugar nor pork and very little fruit, leaning heavily on legumes, vegetables, and meats. Our meal, a veritable feast, was a pizza-sized *injera* topped with no less than six meat dishes and various vegetable stews, making us feel terribly gluttonous. Like everyplace, the Asmara served fresh juices and cappuccino. An Art Deco-era cappuccino maker issued frothy brew with belabored sounds. It had huge black knobs, the name GAGGIA scrawled across the backside in metal letters, and looked more like a jet engine than a coffee machine.

Two *ferenji* men, a German and a Norwegian, sat at a table kitty-corner to us. They invited us to join them for an after dinner drink. The German had the brutish presence of a big time wrestler, and strutted down Asmara's streets as if he owned the place. The Norwegian, by comparison, demonstrated a kinder, gentler aura. He was passing through Asmara en route from Ethiopia, where he had made a pilgrimage back to the Ethiopian town in which he lived as a child some twenty-odd years earlier. Our newly formed cluster settled into couches at the Keren Hotel bar and conversed rather stiltedly.

The German announced loudly, "You know African drivers!"

A group of young Eritreans sitting nearby looked our way. Kate and I cringed.

"I don't go anywhere you can't get a drink," he guffawed, blowing cigar smoke in Kate's face. "And other things too," he added with a nauseating wink.

Kate and I furnished some excuses, made a quick getaway, and berated ourselves for not being more discriminating.

I took Kate for a nightcap at Bar Adulis. In the back room we drank Melotti beers that arrived at our table in stubby brown bottles—with no labels, as usual. A wretched child entered the room selling plastic photoholder key chains. We laughed at the silly snapshots of heavily made-up Arabic models and bought a few. Some minutes later two men seated on a low couch against the rear wall sent peanuts over to us, distributed by another ragged child merchant.

"Thank you for helping our people," one of the spindly men said, referring to our purchases. Once more, Eritrean generosity proved overwhelming.

This was the perfect setting to recount for Kate the tale of my first night in Eritrea drinking at this same animated joint with Samson and Medhani. As I was concluding the story, I grabbed Kate's arm and told her to turn around quickly and look. There he was: as if on cue, the crazy man had entered the front room of the bar and was charging toward the petite owner sitting on a barstool. The man dropped to his knees and bit the owner's ankle.

\* \* \*

Early in the morning, Kate and I boarded a northbound bus to Massawa, Eritrea's second largest city after Asmara, and the country's main port. Lauded for good snorkeling and pristine beaches, Massawa is a popular weekend destination for locals and the smattering of foreign residents. Like Keren, Massawa is 65 miles (105 kilometers) from Asmara, only this time the bus would descend from 7,765 feet (2,300 meters) to sea level in about four hours.

Despite the fact that there are no set departure times—or maybe because of it—the bus system in Eritrea is orderly and efficient. The bus arrives at the station, passengers place their bags on the seat of their choice, then they either sit on the bus and wait or retire to a shady place nearby to drink tea. When every seat is filled, one person to each seat, the bus leaves.

The journey down the Arbe-Robu'e escarpment is like an ungainly ballet—cars rush down the slopes teetering in the outer lane, trucks chug slowly upward clinging to the mountainsides, bus passengers sway side to side as coaches negotiate the hairpin turns.

Dropping from a cool highland plateau to steamy coastal plains, the air in the bus swiftly became hot and sticky. The essence of Eritrea's tourism slogan Three Seasons in Two Hours eluded me. In Asmara it felt like Ohio in springtime; approaching the coast it became Florida in August. But I felt no third season, and our trip was taking closer to four hours than two. Perhaps the slogan could be revised for bus travelers: Two Seasons (One Splendid, One Sweltering) in Four (Really Long) Hours. And my young friend Haben, who pulls tourists off the streets to visit his unsupervised home, could be the poster child. Actually, a tour company called Bicycle Africa Tours has devised the best variation on the slogan: "three seasons, three millenniums, and three thousand vertical."

From the bus window I could see road works were underway and national service encampments had been erected on sun-baked cliffs. I wondered if that assignment would be considered an unlucky draw. Certainly, the luckier ones are those who do national service while remaining in their field of expertise. For instance, the manager of the Keren Hotel told me that he studied hotel management in Germany. His national service consisted of working at a government hotel for two years.

"Some fight," he explained. "Some do this."

As usual, the bus's stereo speakers were distorted and the music had that repetitive, pounding beat that I had grown to hate in Keren.

"Such a great country," said Kate. "Such bad music."

She catches on quickly. I passed one of my home-mixed cassette tapes to the bus tout. The tape led with Keola Beamer, a Hawaiian slack key guitarist whose songs once had a lovely calming affect on my nieces and nephews at home. But, when blared through defective speakers, Keola Beamer sounded like substandard Musak. My cassette was, however, tolerable and tolerated. That is, until Canada's latest angst-ridden diva Alanis Morissette began screeching the lurid words of a hard-driving rock song. Passengers snatched sideways glances at one another. Kate and I sank down into our bench seat. The driver signaled to the tout to switch the music off and silence became the compromise for the remainder of the journey.

In a stroke of luck, the bus dropped us off right behind the Dhalak Hotel. Rachel, my photographer companion from Keren, had traveled down to Massawa a few days earlier and had already booked a room for us. Massawa encompasses two islands and two peninsulas. The Dhalak Hotel sits on the edge of the first island, Twalet, and overlooks a bay and causeway leading to the second island, Batsa'e. Boasting the largest natural deep-water port on the Red Sea, Batsa'e is also home to a fascinating Turko-Egyptian old town.

In Asmara, with the exception of the occasional disabled veteran tooling around in a three-wheel motorized wheelchair, one can easily forget that the country just emerged from three decades of war. But in Massawa, the violent past becomes unavoidable. From February 1990 until the country's liberation in May 1991, Massawa underwent extensive shelling and bombing by Ethiopian forces. Gaping cavities in buildings, piles of rubble, and bullet-pocked walls make for a haunting greeting upon the approach to the city. Overlooking the causeway to Batsa'e, the old Imperial Palace is perhaps the most disturbing reminder of the destructive nature of war. Once the winter retreat of Ethiopian Emperor Haile Selassie, the palace now has a huge chunk blown from its metallic dome and much of its facade has crumbled, melting back to its original sixteenth century foundations. When the war began in the 1960s, Massawa was a thriving port city of 80,000; today only about 20,000 residents remain.

*The causeway to Massawa*

*Donkeys and cars share the causeway to Massawa*

*The ghibi or palace at Massawa, destroyed by war*

With temperatures in Massawa typically around 100 degrees Fahrenheit (38 degrees Celsius), and sometimes reaching 115, the first order of business is water—getting into it. We easily accepted the Dhalak Hotel's complimentary motorboat ride to Sheikh Said Island, known to tourists as Green Island or Isola Verde, a tiny islet in the bay visible from the hotel. After disembarking and rounding a sandy bend, we saw Rachel strolling down the beach toward us, her boyish body exposed in a cutout one piece swimsuit.

"My own private island," she called out and waved.

The sea was so shallow on the far side of the island that it prohibited any full on swimming, so we dropped into the warm water and wallowed around like hippos. Birds squawked and flapped on the beach and overhead, while schools of jumping fish made more racket than a high school swim team practicing the butterfly stroke.

The brother of a British friend from Nairobi lived in Massawa and worked for the Marine Resources Department. He, his wife, and their two children met us on the hotel veranda for a drink at sunset. Not an overly gregarious family, they complained about the "cool" season—meaning temperatures between sixty-five and ninety degrees Fahrenheit.

"It brings the four plagues," the parents told us, "flies, mosquitoes, aid workers, and tourists."

Under the veil of night, even destruction and decay can be enchanting. The full moon glowed through vast holes in a bombed out building near the port. Brilliant white spotlights from docked ships irradiated the sky. Spits of amber lantern light revealed fragments of ancient splendor: chiseled stone lintels, heavy beams suspending high-ceilings, a stairway winding to a rooftop, a second-story latticed bay window, the skeleton of a wooden roof that once covered a narrow street. I could imagine a velvet-robed Turkish Khedive standing beneath the peaked arch of a balcony, stoically surveying the streets below.

On Saturday night Massawa town buzzes and the smells are marvelous. Women lounge on wooden stools outside their homes roasting coffee beans over charcoal and, as is customary, burning frankincense in small clay pots. One-room grocery stores remain open into the night, their shelves stacked with colorful boxes and tins reaching up to the ceiling, and single-room fabric stores brim with dazzling materials and garments. The neon sign maker knelt in the street outside his shop putting the finishing touches on a piece of work. It appeared he does a roaring business. Any store with a modicum of success has one of his luminous signs, causing Massawa to glow at night like a state fair. Even the government building behind the Dhalak Hotel advertised its services with a large neon sign, and its roof was rung with multicolored neon lights.

At outdoor cafes bordering open squares, men sip sweet steamy tea from small glasses or drink ice cold water out of perspiring aluminum cups. Dogs wander

*Kate enjoys fresh juice at an outdoor cafe in Massawa*

around the rubble-strewn earthen streets growling at each other. Through windows and doors cracked open to yield to the tepid night air, one can catch glimpses of the intimate side of local life. In single-room dwellings the bed is the main feature, and pots and pans hang on the walls as practical decorations. People sit on stools inside drinking coffee or tea and conversing with friends. One family fortunate enough to own a television left their door swung open so that a small crowd of neighbors could pull up chairs or stand outside and watch. An old man standing in a doorframe wore a silly hat made from an express mail document package. His two friends laughed when we pointed after noticing him. The hatman became totally embarrassed, as if he had agreed to some sort of a dare.

As visitors, we felt more anonymous in Massawa than in Asmara. Residents, surely more accustomed to tourists, both Eritrean and foreign, are less giddy about guests to their city. Nonetheless, we found a college student from Asmara University named Tewelde who happily guided us through the old town's windy streets to the Salaam Fish Restaurant. Nothing more than a collection of tables and chairs strewn in a dirt street, this popular restaurant attracts locals and foreigners. The waiters plop heavily spiced whole fish, heads and tails draping over the edges of plastic plates, in front of diners. The fish is accompanied by *chapatis* (a flat Indian bread), lime wedges, and beer. Underneath the tables, bony cats scavenge for scraps.

Although there are not many places to swim in Massawa as yet, there will be soon enough. The Eritrean government intends to pursue tourism as one path toward economic development, and Massawa and its environs certainly will be a focus of this effort. With the assistance of the United Nations Development Program and the World Tourism Organization, plans for a tourism school in Asmara were underway. An American company had ambitions to spend US $200 to US $300 million constructing a casino-resort complex on Dhalak Kebir Island, the largest of the 354 sparsely-inhabited pristine islands off the Eritrean coastline. This resort complimented the country's bid to attract tourists from the Arabian peninsula. Two Australian aid workers riding on our bus had seen the plans for the resort. The women shook their heads at the thought of "red slippery slides" and swimming areas segregating women and children from the men.

The main swimming destination for now was Gurgusum Beach, located on the mainland a few miles north of Massawa town. Gurgusum looks like the setting of an Italian movie—perhaps Visconti's *Death in Venice*—with striped red-and-yellow and blue-and-yellow umbrellas in neat rows flapping in the wind. Two Rashaida herdsmen led their ornately decorated camels up and down the beach beckoning tourists to take a ride. Like Green Island, the sea was shallow a long way out and felt like bath water. Once past a barrier of seaweed, however, the bottom was silky smooth.

Most of the bathers were Eritreans. Women wore underpants under ill-fitting swimsuits. One woman skipped into the ocean in stretch pants and a T-shirt, while another swam in shorts and a black brassiere. A skinny boy's cotton underwear, weighed down by the salt water, repeatedly fell off in the waves exposing his little chocolate bum. He later walked up the beach cupping his hands over his crotch, a victim of the wet T-shirt syndrome. Overall, the Eritreans were having one hell of a good time laying on their beach and frolicking in their sea.

Aficionados claim some of the best scuba diving in the world can be done in the Red Sea offshore of the Dhalak Islands. In fact, the waters along the Eritrean coast have been nicknamed "fish soup" because of the 1,000 or so species that live in them. But scuba diving in Eritrea involves chartering a boat and renting equipment if you haven't brought your own. It also requires ample time. Kate, Rachel, and I were only in Massawa for a few days so we went a lower-key route, choosing to snorkel in the bay.

The prefab home of my friend's brother, where snorkeling gear could be rented, was a short walk from our hotel. But it took us more than a half-hour to find it because we relied on a group of barefoot children, one little girl leading a pet monkey around on a leash, for directions. Smiling big angelic smiles and pointing with absolute certainty, the children sent us the completely wrong way. Finally, arriving at the brother's marine resources office-cum-home, we rented snorkeling equipment and splashed around in the bay. On a rocky protrusion nearby I saw amongst a group of Eritrean boys a couple of Asian men fishing.

"The Chinese are building the Red Sea Hotel, the Koreans a housing complex across the water," explained the brother's wife.

I snorkeled solo for several hours in the afternoon, as Kate decided to return to the hotel with Rachel who had to make an early departure for Asmara. Swimming all alone in a sea, even a bay, is a liberating experience. However, snorkeling in that part of the bay was not very remarkable. There were some interesting fish, but nothing sensational in terms of coral.

Earlier, I had slipped on the cement boat ramp getting into the water and cut my hand, and it looked as if it was getting infected despite several hours of snorkeling in salt water. Apparently that wasn't so unusual; Massawa's hot, moist climate was a playground for pathogenic micro-organisms. I recalled that the Italian cook at the Dhalak Hotel, who spoke little English, had his leg wrapped because of a nasty infection. He had looked down at his bandaged knee, shook his head, and said by way of explanation, "Massawa." And an American resident we had chatted with at the bay contemplated whether or not to snorkel because his knee had also been infected for weeks.

\* \* \*

The bus passed through a dense fog on the way back to Asmara. Kate and I could not see beyond the windshield, and we were nervously hopeful that the driver was able to see a bit farther. Surely the power of suggestion had a lot to do with it, but it felt as though the minute the bus started climbing back up the escarpment into the cooler, dryer highlands, my hand began to heal. Moving at a snail's pace up the hills, we saw an overturned truck and an abandoned smashed pickup. A woman with a permanent grin sat across the aisle from us with three children. We told her how cute her baby was, but soon ate our words. The mother held the infant by its underarms, its toes scraping the floor of the aisle, and shook as she commanded "p..p..p." Eeewww. We kicked our bags further under our legs and away from the aisle. Earlier, when boarding the bus, we had noticed a tiny pile of poop on the seat behind us. I suppose it wouldn't be totally false to claim that Eritrean buses are equipped with toilet facilities.

*   *   *

By then we were resigned to Eritrean music and began to take perverse pride in recognizing different songs. "Mun, mun, mun," we hummed, and "Alula." A fighter (a ubiquitous term Eritreans use for former soldiers of the liberation army) was sitting beside us, leaning against the window. He proffered sticks of gum.

"No, thanks," we both replied.

"Why not?" he demanded.

Kate accepted a piece and tore it in half.

"So as not to insult," she whispered and handed a half to me. A small attractive man, the fighter said he joined the rebels when he was just twelve years old. They schooled him for five years and then, at the age of seventeen, he began fighting. Now twenty-nine, he told us that he taught Tigrinya language in the army.

The bus stopped for lunch at Ghinda, a roadside town in a productive agricultural belt, indicating that we had traveled half the distance back to Asmara. The fighter led us across a muddy raised walkway to a cafe. I ordered a box of juice and reached into my pocket for some *birr*. The fighter grabbed my wrist firmly and held my arm away from my purse while he handed the cashier the three *birr* that it cost. There was no stopping him from also treating us to a plate of spaghetti. I felt guilty; veteran fighters in the 40,000-member Eritrean army, I had read, made only US $25 a month. As the three of us sauntered out of the cafe, a fellow passenger ran up, excitedly babbling something to the effect of, "What the heck are you doing? The bus is leaving without you!" Apparently, the bus had actually started driving away and the passengers all yelled for the driver to stop and wait for us. Mind-boggling generosity had become the theme in Eritrea.

Kate and I recognized that we had not scheduled enough time for the Pearl of the Red Sea, as Massawa was known. Would any amount of time have been enough, I wondered? But Ethiopia beckoned.

# Family
# Meal

*Enjoy life before
you have a child.*

— Eritrean maxim

The spirit of a city and of its people is directly related to one's own disposition. With only one day left in Asmara, I felt pressed and irritable. So many wonderful people to see before leaving; so much shopping and shipping to do. A clerk at a silver shop was outright curt: Her body language screamed, "Hurry up and choose, would you." Employees at the Ambassador Hotel, lacking their usual broad grins, also seemed to be in foul moods. They could see I was perturbed that, for the second time in one day, an empty cardboard box that I had scrounged from a nearby bookstore for shipping gifts home had disappeared under their care. Nonetheless, as usual, they aimed to please and quickly furnished another box.

Another great aspect of Eritrea is the ability to send packages home hassle free. Whereas in Nairobi this same chore would have involved several frustrating hours of cue standing, shoving, and bribery, in Asmara it was downright fun. At the back of the post office is the shipping office. There is no line and there are no customers, just a few sweet-tempered customs officers awaiting business. Show the women the items you intend to ship, pack and seal them in their presence, carry the box to the shipping window, and pay the airmail fee. That easy!

The customs clerks wanted to discuss my souvenirs. They all stood up to examine a traditional Tigrinya dress and to inquire how much I paid.

"Good price," they assured me.

These aren't customs officers, I thought, they're shopping police. The women saw that my box included a *djellabia* for my boyfriend at home.

"You must take a picture of you and your husband in these clothes," said the ladies, "and send us a copy."

I promised I would, as if by sending a picture to the post office, like tossing a coin over a turned shoulder into Rome's Fountain of Trevi, it might guarantee my return one day to Asmara.

\*   \*   \*

Amleset was thrilled that I had arranged for Kate, the Canadian, and a compatriot of her children, to meet her and her family. She led us by the hand from her office at the Catholic Cathedral to her home. Amleset's youngest son Aron, recently returned home from national service, greeted the three of us as we entered the high steel security gate surrounding their compound.

"Welcome to our house." Aron handed me a bouquet of fresh flowers.

By American standards, Amleset's home was modest. One room served as the parents' bedroom. Over a large wooden bed hung a rug printed with a picture of Jesus.

"She sleeps with him I think," said Aron, teasing his mother for her devoutness.

Amleset hid her head in embarrassment as Aron continued our tour: next a cramped kitchen, a small bathroom, and a living room divided in two by a circular archway and a violet floral-patterned curtain. The living room walls were painted rose and mint green and the wooden door and window frames that ever-popular baby blue. Concrete tiles covered the floor. In the front half of the living room, Amleset had meticulously arranged gold yarn doilies on the backs of the couch and chairs. Against one wall, a single bed with a shimmering pink bedspread doubled as Aron's bedroom and visitor seating.

The evening began slowly. Amleset stayed busy in the kitchen cooking *injera*, meat stew, and *shiro*, tossing salad. Aron ran back and forth, dividing his time between entertaining the guests and helping his mother in the kitchen. In the meantime, Kate and I drank ample amounts of *mes* while browsing through family photo albums. There were pictures of recent trips to Massawa and to Israel, as well as old family photos. From the photographs, we could see that the bluish cross tattooed on Amleset's forehead had been present since she was a little girl. Amleset was beautiful in her youth and her husband had the countenance of a Hollywood movie star. Theirs was an arranged marriage; Amleset had not met her husband beforehand but he had seen her, she explained and smiled. As Amleset would say, they were lucky, God blessed them. Amleset's most prized possession is a certificate in recognition of their twenty-fifth wedding anniversary, signed by the Pope.

Friends and relatives filtered in off the streets to welcome Aron back from national service. Amleset rushed around, ever the conscientious hostess. Everyone who entered the house was swiftly presented with food and drink. A neighbor, a boy of about five or six years old, spent the entire evening sitting silently on a low stool. He was allotted a bowl of salad and a breadloaf, which he ate absentmindedly as his large brown eyes followed the activity in the room. Two robust women about Amleset's age, their heads

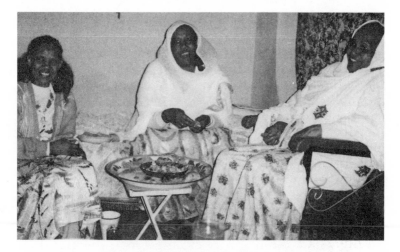

*Amleset and friends sharing a meal*

*Amleset, Mebratu, and Kate helping to make traditonal-style coffee*

covered by gauze shawls, sat down across the room on Aron's bed. Amleset brought them pint-sized metal cups of *suwa*, a home-brewed beer that looks—and some say tastes—like muddy water, and a large tray of *injera* topped with *shiro* and green salad, but no meat stews like she had served to other guests.

"Something religious," explained Aron off-handedly.

Although we couldn't understand the precise wording, it was clear that these women were bossing around Amleset and all the youngsters.

"Fill mine up," one appeared to command Amleset, who leapt up and poured more *suwa* into the woman's cup. The other buxom woman similarly berated Aron for not filling her shot glass of *Zebib* to the tiptop.

Amleset's husband arrived home late. Kate said she would introduce her single brother to his daughter Zufan who lived in Toronto. "Take her!" he said with a laugh.

As I understood it, this jovial family originally lived in Massawa. They were forced by the war to run away from their home. They walked for one and a-half months, with four children, to reach Keren town where some relatives lived.

"The Eritrean Front," Amleset said, her voice lowered, I suspect out of habit, "gave us food, even when they themselves were hungry. But, thanks God, we all were fine."

She said they were all fine, but she and her husband spent two months in a hospital in Asmara recovering their strength while a grandmother in Keren looked after their children.

My camera was greeted enthusiastically. Like many other Africans, Eritreans love photos; in fact, having studio portraits taken is a national obsession. We took turns shooting pictures of Amleset, Kate, and myself. The matriarchs ordered Amleset to sit on a pillow.

"You are too short," they stormed. "You look like a child next to them."

Amleset hauled out her traditional Tigrayan dress, a white cotton gown with golden embroidery around the cuffs and down the front in the shape of a cross.

*The author wearing Amleset's traditional dress*

She said that these beautiful garments are worn as wedding dresses. Amleset instructed me to put on the flowing dress and pose for photos. Her husband dragged over a four-foot plastic Christmas tree, while Amleset ran off to grab an arrangement of colorful satin flowers. The husband threw himself into several of the shots, linking arms with me.

"It is our wedding photo!" he shouted through the laughter. "Our marriage!"

The same event was repeated in its entirety with Kate now the center of attention.

"Thanks God, we find each other, Julie," Amleset repeated several times as Kate and I rose to leave.

She was thrilled that I had brought Kate to her, a connection—no matter how nebulous—to her children in Canada. Aron and a friend named Yohannes drove us back to the Ambassador Hotel. They joined us for a drink in the hotel's upstairs bar. I had not noticed until then that Aron was not drinking any alcohol.

"I'm an athlete," he explained.

Our two young escorts were sure to grow only more sweet and handsome in the coming years. We quizzed them about girlfriends.

"He is my boyfriend and my girlfriend." Aron laughed and nodded towards Yohannes. "He works, I do sport. We don't have time for girlfriends."

I began to recognize a rather uncommon trend for an African capital—urbanites delaying marriage and childrearing to later ages. I recalled that the fighter on the bus from Massawa acted surprised when Kate and I asked if he was married after he told us he was twenty-nine. Neither Samson nor Medhani, whom I would guess to be in their late twenties, were married, and none of the Kelete children, all in their twenties and thirties, were married or had children.

Aron knocked at the door of my hotel room at 6:40 the next morning. He was carrying three kilos of spices for Kate to transport to Amleset's daughter in Toronto and wanted to bid us farewell. I was tired and wrung out; I am no "athlete," and thus had drunk too much *mes*, *zebib*, and Melotti beer at Amleset's house the night before. But I was a happy earthling. Eritrea, in some respects, was the way I had dreamed all of Africa might be one fine day. Never in my life had I felt a greater sense of community on a national scale. Nor had I seen a place with such wide-open arms and so generous a heart. I pronounced Eritrea my favorite country on earth.

"You and everyone else," a friend told me later.

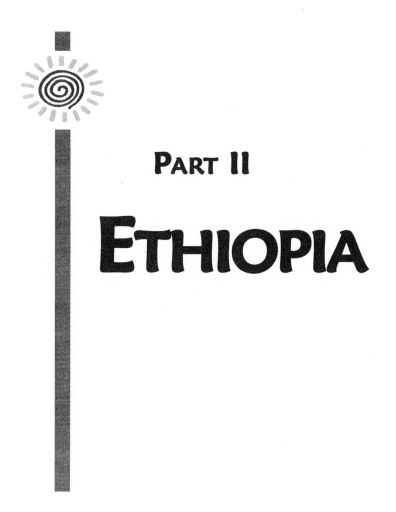

# PART II

# ETHIOPIA

# Historical Background

Writing in 1955, author John Gunther called Ethiopia "an impregnable feudal kingdom lost in space." The country has come a long way in forty years—from empire, to Marxist dictatorship, through a thirty-year war with Eritrea, to emerging democracy.

Formerly known as Abyssinia, the name Ethiopia is Greek for "burnt face." Rather round shaped, Ethiopia is the twenty-first largest country in the world. With a total area of 435,184 square miles (1,127,127 square kilometers) it is almost double the size of Texas or the size of France, Spain, and Portugal combined.

Ethiopia's position a few degrees north of the equator accounts for the sun's relentlessness, but its high plateaus and mountain ranges mitigate the heat, giving rise to the nickname the Land of Perennial Spring.

Ethiopian history started to take shape, as noted in Part I, when the Axumite Kingdom in modern Ethiopia's northern Tigray Province arose in the first century AD and developed into a powerful trading kingdom. The growth of Islam in the seventh century forced the Christian Axumites deep into the Ethiopian highlands, where they remained largely insular for almost one thousand years. By the Twelfth century, with the ascendancy of the Zagwe Dynasty, the Axumite Kingdom moved its administrative center even further south into Ethiopia.

The Solomonic line came to the fore in 1270, with King Menelik I basing his authority to rule on descendance from the biblical union of King Solomon of Jerusalem and Queen Sheba of Ethiopia. Under the Solomonic line, the kingdom expanded its territories and, with the aid of Portuguese soldiers in the 1500s, repelled Mohammedan invasions.

The Oromo people (today Ethiopia's largest ethnic group) migrated from the southwest in the mid sixteenth century and integrated into the army and the imperial government, as well as into the royal family and the nobility. The following two centuries became known as Zamana Masafint, the Era of the Princes, a period marked by decentralized control and incessant civil war.

In the mid-1800s, the son of a minor chieftain declared himself king and with the crowning of Tewodros II, the Solomonic line was restored. Tewodros II successfully subdued the independent kingdoms of Amhara, Gojjam, Tigre, and Shoa. Yohannes IV (1872-1889) and Menelik II (1889-1913) followed Tewodros II. Menelik II prevented Italy from seizing Ethiopia, his 90,000 troops thoroughly routing a 13,000-strong Italian army at the 1896 Battle of Adowa. To this day, Ethiopians revere Adowa. They also like to remind a forgetful world that Ethiopia is the only African nation never to have been colonized. (From 1936-1941 Mussolini's forces occupied Ethiopia, but the

Italians were ousted at the beginning of WWII by native and British forces.) The Battle of Adowa might also be viewed as sowing the seeds of discontent in the Tigray region: Menelik dispatched his imperial troops to the north without adequate provisions, forcing soldiers to pillage from local towns and villages for survival.

In 1928, Ethiopia's last king was crowned. Born Tafari Mekonnen, he became known as Haile Selassie I, the "Conquering Lion of the Tribe of Judah, Elect of God, and King of Kings of Ethiopia." Haile Selassie ruled until the mid-1970s, well into the days when kingdoms—in the old feudal sense—had become obsolete. During his half-century reign, Haile Selassie attempted to modernize the kingdom. He established ties with European nations, professionalized the army and police force, established a public school system, and founded a university. With Selassie's support waning internally and globally, in 1974 a group of military personnel known as the Derg took over the palace and put the emperor under house arrest.

A closed council of military officers, the Derg's secretive inner workings were completely unknown to outsiders and no new members were admitted over the thirteen years of its existence. The Derg's first several years were marked by infighting, including a shootout in 1977 at the Grand Palace in Addis Ababa during which Mengistu Haile Mariam's supporters literally shot him to the top of the Derg's hierarchy. Mengistu led the country for the next decade and a half. He set up a socialist system with a strong central government. The government took over private industries, commercial agriculture, rental properties, and financial institutions. Under the rubric of Marxism-Leninism, the Mengistu regime received financial aid and military backing from the Soviet Union and its allies, North Korea and Cuba.

The Mengistu era was a bleak period in Ethiopian history. A bloody "reign of terror" ensued against the government's real and perceived political enemies. In the mid-1980s, weather conditions, insect plagues, and government policies that decreased agricultural production combined to create one of the most horrific calamities of the modern age—the great Ethiopian famine. The government resettled peasants from drought-prone (and rebel-prone) northern regions to more fertile areas in the south and southwest. From 1985 to 1986, an estimated 600,000 people were forcibly removed from their farms and homes by the military and sent to southern regions of the country. Human rights organizations claimed that tens of thousands died as a result of the resettlement scheme.

Civil war raged in the north in Tigray and Eritrea. Ultimately, these civil wars were Mengistu's undoing. By 1991, Eritrea's EPLF and the Tigray-based EPRDF had victory in their sights. The EPLF marched into Asmara on May 24, and the EPRDF took Addis Ababa on May 27 and 28, as Mengistu fled to Zimbabwe. The EPRDF and its thirty-six year old leader Meles Zenawi had seized a sinking ship: government coffers were empty, seven million people teetered on the threshold of starvation, the gross domestic product (GDP) was declining, and inflation was rising. International coffee prices had plunged, while defense spending was eating up nearly forty percent of the national budget. According to World Bank classifications at the time, Ethiopia was the world's poorest country.

Ethiopia's nascent government set its sights on the difficult task of reversing the country's cataclysmic decline. By July 1991, Eritrea's EPLF had agreed with the EPRDF to make Assab and Massawa free ports for Ethiopia in exchange for a referendum on Eritrean self-determination. Privatization of public holdings commenced. Ethiopia adopted a federal system of government and was divided into twelve autonomous regions based on ethnic identity and two chartered cities for all ethnicities, Addis Ababa and Harar.

According to World Bank press releases, by 1996 Ethiopia had a modest food surplus, the GDP experienced a 7.6 percent annual growth rate, and military spending was being shifted into human resource budgets. Things are looking up these days for this tortured land. But, despite considerable gains, as we will see, life is still far from utopia in Ethiopia.

# Addis
# Ababa

*The smile of a dog and the deeds of God, one does not understand.*

— Oromo proverb

Just as driving tends to bring out aggressive behavior in people, so do African airports. Ethiopian Airways allowed open seating on the route from Asmara to Addis Ababa, so these normally orderly people jockeyed for positions in line like children in the school cafeteria on pizza day. In hindsight, why we pushed and shoved each other onto a plane headed for Ethiopia's capital rather than bolting back into our taxi and driving straight back to Asmara, I'll never know.

Addis Ababa, wrote John Gunther in 1955 in *Inside Africa,* looked as though it had been "dropped piecemeal from an airplane carrying trash." Things haven't changed too much. As our jet approached the city, I could see an endless plain of gleaming tin rooftops stretched out below. Over ninety percent of the homes in Addis Ababa have corrugated metal roofs and more than fifty percent have earthen floors.

While Asmara was a small town, Gunther noted forty years earlier, Addis Ababa was a big village. Located in the center of the country, Addis Ababa remains part big village, but also part reckless, overgrown city. It has become an octopus on a plateau—the downtown high-rise buildings its body, the suburban extensions its tentacles. Blocked by the Entoto Mountains to the north, the city's tentacles go unchecked to the south, grasping for an illusive sea. But the creature will never find salt water: Addis Ababa, at 7,868 feet (2,400 meters), is the fourth highest capital city in the world (after La Paz, Bogota, and Quito), and is hundreds of miles from any coast.

Planning must be an alien and hostile concept to Ethiopians. Addis Ababa is like *spris*—tossed together in a blender. Multistory buildings compete with shacks for street-front property. Behind our hotel stood mud and wattle huts straight out of a pastoral African scene; in front rose modern high rises and a chaotic, traffic-filled street. Just as the lines between urban and rural are blurred, so are distinctions between affluent and impoverished neighborhoods. According to the UN's *Global Report on Human Settlements*, an incredible seventy-nine percent of the city's four to six million people are inadequately housed or homeless.

Upon first examination, the city's name Addis Ababa—"new flower" in Amharic—is completely incongruous, for throngs of destitute give the place a ghastly, not floral, air. Rows of indigent Ethiopians, swathed in lengths of soiled cotton cloth, line the perimeter walls of city churches. Some with bodies grotesquely distorted, they squat on concrete sidewalks and beg, or just sit with their backs pressed against the tall walls. As citizens of better fortune walk by, needy mothers push toddlers into their path, forcing their tiny outstretched hands into a pitiful plea.

Like the two-dimensional characters in traditional Ethiopian art, the residents of Addis walk their streets with solemn expressions, their thoughts kept to themselves behind enormous brown eyes. Younger ones descend on foreigners commanding, "You! You! You!" They thrust out milk chocolate arms hoping for money, pens, or whatever odd item the tourist will supply, even if it is just a moment or two of abuse. Feeling as though I was walking through a Dali painting, the word "surreal" kept churning through my mind and spilling out of my mouth.

Our first tourism target, based on information from Kate's guide book, was the Piazza, the old center of Addis Ababa, and nearby Saint George's Church with its beautiful stained glass windows. Kate and I imagined discovering a quaint, Italianesque corner of the city, in which we would sip frothy cappuccinos while observing fashionable pedestrians as they sauntered by. The minibus dropped us at the Piazza stop. Hmmm. We looked around for something resembling an Italian-style piazza.

"Is this the Piazza?" we asked several locals.

Yes, they all assured us we had arrived. The Piazza is a congested, noisy taxi and bus park that makes a mockery of its station on a scenic hilltop. There may have been, during a more lavish era, some sort of cool green park at the center of a grand public square. But these days the epicenter of the Piazza is a big grassless plot, where city kids stir up dust playing soccer, surrounded by ramshackle shops frequented by every breed of shady character.

Kate paused to examine a two-story wooden building and its lattice-covered balcony. Most likely it was constructed around the turn of the century during the reign of Emperor Menelik II, when such structures were popular in Addis Ababa. The paint was chipping and the balcony dangled above the sidewalk just daring pedestrians to pass underneath.

"Some of these buildings are charming," Kate chimed.

"Oh, really," I scowled, feeling besieged with resentment at having agreed to come to this God-forsaken country.

Not generally a curmudgeon, my devilish temper surprised even me.

We made our way to Castelli's Restaurant, the place we had imagined sipping cappuccinos streetside. Castelli's, mercifully, had no intention of letting Addis's rank street life spoil its pomp and grandeur. Passing through an indistinct entryway, the city was miraculously transformed from an urchin's playground to a haven of elegance and refinement. Inside Castelli's, rich wooden planks covered the floors and ceilings and ran halfway up the walls. The tables were set with crisp linen, shiny silverware, and fresh flowers. Separate small rooms allowed for an intimate dining experience. The waiters, impeccable in white jackets, spoke both English and Italian. A mouth-watering salad buffet—which appeared nothing short of miraculous in a region that favors meat dishes—had been spread out in the entry room. Our bliss at wallowing in luxury was only briefly interrupted by the clamor of an Italian matron storming down the main hallway. Her footsteps thundered, as a team of elderly white-coated waiters followed behind in triangular formation, the whole scene looking terribly colonial. Although costing only twenty dollars for two people, the price of a modest lunch at home, the meal was an indulgence in this corner of the world.

After only a few hours of walking around the city's filthy streets and crossing over several foul-smelling rivulets, my socks were blackened Cajun-style. In our urban wanderings, Kate and I jumped to the rash conclusion that Addis Ababa was Kampala meets Rome meets Bombay.

"It is not like India," an Eritrean acquaintance had warned us earlier, "but almost."

Two years after this visit, I would read an article in an Ethiopian newspaper, *The Monitor,* calling Addis Ababa an "open air urinal." Despite Eritrea and Ethiopia being so close to each other both geographically and culturally, we were having trouble processing the profound differences, particularly between their capital cities. Kate found Addis Ababa "intimidating" as compared with Asmara, while I kept thinking, thank goodness Eritrea won the war.

A middle-aged American couple Kate and I ran into at Addis Ababa's Bole Airport suggested we stay at the Holiday Hotel on Asmara Road. This was the same couple who had asked us at the airport:

"First time in Addis?"

"Yes," we both said.

"Hold on to your bags," they warned.

"At the airport?" I asked for clarification.

"Everywhere," they replied ominously.

Upon returning from our first foray into the city, we discovered this couple sitting on a couch in the Holiday Hotel lobby having a drink. They were in the process of E.T.ing—terminating early from the Peace Corps. Both held inordinately negative views about their eight months living in Ethiopia.

"There are good people here," the husband explained, "but there are so many who aren't, that it makes it difficult."

They told us stories about problems they'd experienced at their site and about children lobbing stones at foreigners. Whatever doubts I might have had about this couples' objectivity, on this last point I could concur. Earlier, along Churchill Avenue, the main north-south commercial thoroughfare, Kate and I walked past boys playing soccer in an access road. A little boy who was sitting on a curb watching reached over and grabbed my leg. Walking purposefully and talking, Kate and I did not bother to stop or acknowledge the boy. Next thing we knew a chunk of concrete thumped on the ground behind us.

"There are no tourists here," continued the soon to be ex-Peace Corps volunteers. "There is no reason to come here."

The following day, Sarah, another friend from Nairobi, would arrive to join Kate and me for the Ethiopian leg of our trip. There were reasons to come to Ethiopia, as with anyplace in the world, however remotely related to tourism they might be. Kate wanted to blow off steam after completing a two-year contract with UNICEF's Operation Lifeline Sudan and to get a definitive dose of Africa before moving to New York City. I had come partly due to confusion in an e-mail (Kate wrote that we should meet in Ethiopia and I misread it as Eritrea), and part to further my comprehension of this vast continent. Sarah hoped to take a mental break from a difficult few months of discussing commitment fears with her longtime boyfriend. And if those weren't compelling motivations, Addis Ababa's year round temperature of fifty-nine degrees Fahrenheit and Ethiopia's dramatic terrain, considered among the most spectacular in the world, should have been reasons enough.

* * *

The second day that we plunged into the human soup of Addis, now with three of us, the wretchedness and the beggars began to fade into the background. I started to appreciate the Ethiopian penchant for cheerful colors and gaudy decoration. Shopkeepers employed bright murals to advertise their wares. The outside walls of one bar, in the midst of the urban clutter, had been painted to look like a serene English garden.

To appreciate a city's nuances nothing is better than spending time with someone who lives in it. Sarah, Kate, and I decided to look up Tesfaye, a friend of a friend in Nairobi. Tesfaye is an Eritrean businessman who barrels through Addis Ababa in his car the same way he barrels through life—that is, taking calculated risks with joyous determination. While one of Tesfaye's hands guided the steering wheel, the other cut through the air in wild exclamation as he expounded on his wry theories on life. For example, there was Tesfaye's explanation for the multitude of beggars in Addis Ababa: "The culture encourages it. If you give to beggars, you go to heaven."

Ethiopian Christians fulfill part of their religious duties by doling charity to the needy. And almsgiving is one of five acts to which a practicing Muslim must commit, known as the five pillars of Islam.

"Muslims are supposed to give ten percent of their earnings to the poor, but in fact they give point zero five percent," Tesfaye joked.

Muslims traditionally dispensed forty percent of their income in alms, I once read, but with government taxes eating up a modern Muslim's salary, this amount has been significantly reduced.

Between taking us to the Ethiopian Airlines office to sort out our tickets and to the bank to change dollars into *birr*, Tesfaye zipped off to do an errand, hosting and working simultaneously. Business in Addis Ababa, like the unplanned metropolis itself, is jumbled, with merchants poking their fingers into many pies. Tesfaye told us he was starting a travel agency, but currently his office doubled as an import-export shop. I asked Tesfaye's colleague Jima, who drove around town with us, what he did for a living.

"Anything that makes money," he replied.

Tesfaye told us his father's rags-to-riches story. He began selling eggs on the streets of Addis Ababa, and today can brag that all fifteen of his children have been educated in private schools overseas. Tesfaye's father formerly owned several houses in Asmara, but when the Ethiopians occupied the city, his father was ordered to choose one house in which his family could live; the others would become government property. To house his fifteen children, he chose the largest one, Mariam Ghibi. The government seized Mariam Ghibi anyway and converted it into a prison. And, as the cruel ironies of war would have it, the first person held prisoner in the infamous *Ferenji* Ghibi was Tesfaye's father. I heard a kindred story about a bank manager in Asmara who works in an office directly above his old jail cell. The father of Tesfaye's friend Jima likewise lost many valuable assets during the Mengistu regime.

"Thirty years of progress lost," Jima lamented.

These days, fathers and sons are trying to rebuild their family fortunes. Tesfaye said his father was opening a flour factory, while Tesfaye and Jima were investigating the possibilities of exporting bottled mineral water from Ethiopia into Kenya.

Kate, Sarah, and I sat looking out the picture window of Tesfaye's new ground-level office. The room had been freshly painted and carpeted but lacked decoration. It was a great vantage point for watching the bustling street life near the famous Merkato. Located in the Addis Ketema district in the western part of the city and covering several square miles, the Merkato is reputedly the largest open-air market in Africa. Four massive fairground-style buildings, called the *Aderash*, form the heart of this colossal bazaar. The *Aderash* and a network of outdoor stalls embrace several thousand small shops overflowing with silver and amber jewelry, leather products, coffee, incense, embroidered material, ready-to-wear clothing, gaudy religious icons, and imported goods. One guide to Addis Ababa on the World Wide Web describes the Merkato as "a kind of inland port for central Ethiopia...a key exchange point for grains, pulses, oilseeds, vegetables, and animals and an assembly and distribution center for imports."

Guided by one of Tesfaye's staff, we walked around the Merkato for several hours, the only white faces to be seen. In the *Aderash* we entered a clothing shop that sold, among other things, thick velvet capes with gold brocade embroidery and matching velvet tiaras. These gorgeous capes, fit for royalty, would set you back around US $250. In fact, the capes looked very much like *kaba*, cloaks worn by aristocratic men and women during the days of empire. The shopkeeper told us that these days they serve as wedding apparel for both brides and grooms. She insisted that Kate try one on.

"Beautiful on you," a shopper exclaimed. "Your color!"

This was diametrically opposed to what I was thinking and of what Sarah and Kate agreed on later. We saw ourselves looking particularly colorless and angular, especially amongst those creamy brown, stunningly handsome people whom colonial Europeans nicknamed "fuzzy-wuzzies" because of their soft hair. I realized years go when visiting Thailand, where local men and women alike stared at me and asked to feel my hair, that being exotic is not something inherent to a race; exoticism is merely a function of being different from those around you. Everybody is exotic somewhere in the world, and—as I had discovered earlier at the Ethiopian Embassy in Asmara—we were in that place.

We negotiated the maze of the Merkato's outdoor stalls. Barrels of grain and colorful piles of spices were tended by matronly women. The stall owners eagerly waved us over to sample their merchandise and to teach us the Amharic names of the spices. The Amharic alphabet has 212 letters, with dozens of sounds our mouths could not reproduce. Despite the futility of their efforts, this brief interlude from routine brightened up many a market person's day.

As in Arab cultures, the surrounding streets were divided according to trade. For instance, one street housed row after row of tailors, all men, sewing diligently in the open-air, protected from the harsh sun by shady verandas. Such a profusion of merchandise was for sale in this vast emporium—a place that could put any mall in Orange County to shame—that I found it difficult to comprehend who could afford to buy all those goods. There may have been four million potential shoppers in Addis, but at least 3.2 million of those didn't even have decent housing. In one of the world's most downtrodden countries, where most people survive on little more than twenty-five cents a day and unemployment reaches around thirty percent, how many people can afford a US $250 wedding cape or a US $100 gold necklace?

We made our charge into the Merkato and came out unscathed. There were a few disconcerting moments, however. A boy following Kate said to her, twice: "I kill you with a knife." On one street corner we saw a beggar laying on his stomach, his right leg twisted 180 degrees backward and resting beside his face. For a brief second, this site took even Sarah's breath away. Nairobi-slum-hardened and ever the shopper, Sarah quickly rebounded and continued the search for religious kitsch and local crafts.

Loaded down with souvenirs, we returned to Tesfaye's office quite content to observe the Addis Ketema district hubbub from behind thick plate glass. In the back room Tesfaye conducted business over the telephone, itself a rare commodity. With an estimated one telephone per 500 inhabitants, Ethiopia is among the countries with the fewest telephones per capita in the world.

Children noticed the *ferenji* sitting in the window and stopped to laugh, to express shock, and to blow kisses. Older residents had more subdued reactions. Even a beggar woman and her children seemed much more interested in staring at us and smiling than receiving any *birr* as a result of their outstretched hands in what must be a permanent gesture of need.

"We're only here for money," explained two Eritrean men who sat with us in Tesfaye's office.

They sang the praises of Asmara, with Kate and I chiming in the chorus.

"Addis is dirty and chaotic," the men complained as they gave us a ride back to our hotel.

Driving, as well as walking, followed the every man for himself rule. Pedestrians and cars, by mutual agreement, ignored each other. People walked in the streets even when the sidewalk was empty and cars whizzed by them so closely that there was often only a cat's whisker to spare. Meskal Square, which we had to traverse to get back to our hotel, was a most amazing mishmash of vehicles. Four wide streets converged into a massive central square with no apparent mandate whatsoever. Drivers just squirmed their way through, a little at a time, and somehow the chaos functioned.

A man lay on his side in the middle of the road wriggling like a crushed worm. I wondered out loud if a car had hit him.

"No, he's drunk!" one of the Eritrean businessmen cried. "This is democracy; I have my democratic right to be like this. In Asmara he would be put in jail for a month!"

Our escorts assessed our nationalities: "One U.K., one Canadian, one American. All lucky countries."

It isn't that Ethiopia is an unlucky country, it's just that its luck, like the land, sometimes dries up. With fifty-eight million people, it is the third most populated nation on the African continent, surpassed only by Egypt and Nigeria. Most of this multitude lives in densely packed areas. And eighty-five percent of the inhabitants work in agriculture, according to United Nations Food and Agriculture Organization statistics for 1996, which means that the majority of Ethiopians coax a meager existence out of a stubborn earth.

"Ethiopia is a peasant country," wrote author D.J. Mesfin, "and its heart is in the land." Despite this agricultural bent and the fact that the country has the highest number of head of cattle in Africa—FAO reports 29,900,000 head of cattle in 1996—many of its people are starving. The World Health Organi-zation recommends 2,300 calories per person per day, but the daily available calories in Ethiopia as of 1996, according to a USAID report to Congress, was 1,500-1,600 calories. That is equivalent to the calories in about five cups of Weight Watcher's soup. Ethiopians are not exactly feasting.

Whereas the world's population has doubled since the 1950s, Ethiopia's population has at least trebled and perhaps grown nearly sixfold, depending on the source. On average, according to UN statistics for 1990-95, seven children are born to each Ethiopian woman. Factors such as scarcity of family planning, early marriages, and traditions that adhere to the belief that "the larger the family, the richer you are," combine to aid and abet the rapid skyward climb of Ethiopia's population.

A complaint repeated by foreign residents of Ethiopia was that they found it difficult to make Ethiopian friends. One expatriate couple living in Addis Ababa speculated that Ethiopians shun close association with foreigners because in the past such activity was viewed with suspicion. The couple also suggested that Ethiopians are not entirely confident about the country's current state of peace. I recall that while living in Nairobi, several of my Ethiopian friends always managed to cloak their daily comings and goings in mystery. Whereas I might say, *I am going to have spaghetti for dinner at my friend Sharon's house on Denis Pritt Road,* the Ethiopians would *have to meet some people to take care of some things.*

In *Inside Africa,* author John Gunther quoted one foreigner as saying: "These are the most arrogant people in the world, and this is their most endearing quality." An Ethiopian folktale explaining how God created the different races of mankind lends credence to charges of vanity. When God was making the heavens and the earth he decided to fashion people out of dough. God shoveled the first batch of human cutouts into an oven, but didn't cook them long enough. They came out white and pasty, so he threw them toward the north where they became the people of Europe. Making the second batch, he overcompensated for his error, and the people came out blackened. God tossed them to the south where they became the Bantu people of Africa. By the third batch, God got the temperature and timing just right. He gathered these perfect light-brown people into the palm of his hand and gently set them down on top of the world, in Ethiopia.

While arrogance is a trait not unfamiliar to peoples throughout the Horn of Africa, I have to wonder if Ethiopian aloofness is in part a result of twenty years of harsh communist rule, and centuries of oppressive imperial rule before that, under which leaking too many of your thoughts could produce deadly results. This state of mind is reflected in the Amharic saying, *yaltereteré temeneteré*—he who is not suspicious will be chopped off. It must be hard to break the habit of avoiding giving any public indication as to whether you support one particular party and ideology or another. "They are afraid to talk," observed the Peace Corp volunteer couple.

Polish journalist Ryszard Kapuscinski wrote a moving account of the paranoia-filled latter years of Haile Selassie's reign in *The Emperor: Downfall of an Autocrat.* Kapuscinski's interviewees told of an insanely suspicious emperor who began each day receiving reports from informants, and who kept damning files on his dignitaries. Factions within the royal court played off one another to gain favor with Haile Selassie, who nurtured this divisive game as a way of solidifying power at the top.

Kapuscinski gathered the material for his book clandestinely only a few years after a group of junior army officers toppled Haile Selassie's empire and established a purportedly Marxist-Leninist government. Kapuscinski described Addis Ababa in the late 1970s as a city of fear, crawling with machine gun-mounted jeeps [the forerunner of "technicals" that today terrorize the streets of Mogadishu, the capital city of neighboring Somalia]. This period was characterized by drive-by shootings and overnight disappearances.

The Derg (while the name conjures up images of a hostile race featured on *Star Trek*, it simply means "council" in Amharic), the new government's ruling inner circle, suppressed opposition by providing arms to civilian supporters, leaving them to do their dirty work. But many people armed by the Derg were not Mengistu's disciples after all. Nobody knew whom to trust, so they trusted no one. Residents were subjected to house searches and arbitrary arrest, and mutilated bodies were dumped on roadsides at night. In December 1977, government troops killed one thousand students who had passed out antigovernment leaflets. Another two thousand students and teachers were massacred in 1978. Sources estimate that 30,000 people lost their lives in this fratricide known as the "Red Terror."

In 1937, long before Haile Selassie and Mengistu perfected fear as a tool of governance, occupying Italian forces executed 30,000 Ethiopians, including nearly half of the young educated class, in retaliation for an assassination attempt on the Italian governor.

Ethiopian refugees I knew in Nairobi, when asked why
they had fled to Kenya, would reply simply, "I was a
student." For them—and now for me—that explanation was enough.

Kapuscinski found Ethiopians "deeply distrustful"
and "as silent as the Chinese." Twenty years earlier,
another writer, Oden Meeker in his *Report on Africa*,
called theirs a "mountaineer's distrust." A sinister and
painful political history has heaped layers of suspicion onto this traditional mountaineer's distrust, and
it will likely take a long time to peel away.

*   *   *

A unique aspect of Addis Ababa is the profusion of
restaurants and bars in the front rooms of private
homes, inconspicuously tucked away in residential
back streets. This practice reaches back at least to the
1950s when Meeker estimated that there were several
thousand *tej* joints scattered throughout residential
areas of the city. (*Tej* is homemade honey wine, the
Ethiopian equivalent of Eritrea's *mes*.) As plentiful as
they might be, locating these establishments would be
perplexing without the help of a local.

Tesfaye and his wife Meaza collected us at the
Holiday Hotel and spirited us away to one of these
newly opened speakeasy-style restaurants. Wearing a
fur jacket with a fox head draped over each shoulder,
Meaza looked beautiful. She was tall and willowy, and
had a mole between her eyes that spawned the same
bewitching effect as a *bindi*, the red dot on a married
Hindu woman's forehead that brings good fortune. Her
English was shaky, so she sat quietly, patiently listening to us engaging in rapid conversation.

Tesfaye glanced over at the owner propped on her
elbows behind a half-moon glittery bar: "Nice to have
a bar in your living room." We sat on comfortable
couches arranged around an oversized circular coffee
table. After giving each of us a plate, the hostess
arranged small bowls of *kitfo* around the table. Spiced
ground beef, *kitfo* is a popular meal for well-to-do

Addis Ababa residents. Being able to afford meat is a symbol of wealth and status throughout Africa. In Ethiopia, with the exception of Castelli's, we found vegetable dishes especially hard to come by in upscale restaurants. Ethiopian friends in Nairobi, I recalled, preferred to eat their *kitfo* raw. Consequently, they suffered from tapeworms, and the occasional de-worming process sounded gruesome. Tesfaye assured us that this *kitfo* was well cooked.

Normally the *injera* that accompanies Ethiopian food is served as one large flat bread and diners tear off small pieces to scoop up their food from a communal plate. That night, however, the *injera* had been rolled up and cut into small segments and we all had been given our own plates.

"Why is it cut like this?" I asked Tesfaye.

"Modern style," he replied with a wink.

Like most Westerners who voluntarily spend their lives in so-called Third World countries, I'm drawn to these places in part because they haven't succumbed entirely to modernization. Third World countries function a little more on the edge. Eating with your hands from the same dish as your friends might seem slightly primal, but instead it evokes feelings of shared spirituality. Individual servings of *injera* are more sanitary, I am sure, but I couldn't help but sigh at this creeping sign that the movers and shakers of Addis Ababa were eschewing some of their more engaging cultural ways.

Our last stop for the evening was a backstreet nightclub. The particular one Tesfaye chose, he told us, is a local favorite. A woman whose husband was killed during the Mengistu regime owns it. The couple had owned a restaurant in town, but that closed down after her husband's death. The wife needed means of support, so she set up a bar in her house. The enterprise became so successful that she moved her residence elsewhere. The clubs' rooms were furnished with low cozy chairs and carved wooden coffee tables. A vocalist accompanied by an electric organ belted out songs a bit too loud, as usual. For those needing a breather, outside beside the parking area was a coffee den.

"Ethiopia is a fortress of Christianity surrounded by Muzzies," said Tesfaye.

His description paraphrased the words of Emperor Menelik II who once called Ethiopia "an island of Christians in a sea of Pagans." If a Westerner knows but one fact about Ethiopia, it is that Ethiopians are Christians—which is only half-true. Looking at a map, one can see that Eritrea and Ethiopia are surrounded by Islamic states—Djibouti, Somalia, the Sudan—and are only a short voyage from Mecca, the holiest of all Muslim sites. Like Eritrea, the population of Ethiopia is split approximately fifty-fifty between Sunni Muslims and Christians.

During the tidal wave of Muslim incursions into the region beginning in the seventh century, Ethiopia's impregnable highlands served as refuge for Christian kingdoms and fiefdoms, while around them their neighbors were falling like dominos to Islam. Today, Christians still primarily inhabit the highlands and Muslims the lowlands. Because Ethiopia's Muslims were largely barred from the inner sanctums of imperial power, they adopted the merchant class mantle. While Ethiopia's ruling classes coveted the ranks of nobility, warrior, and priest, they relegating the lowly occupation of trader to Muslims and foreigners, which included many Eritreans.

Roy Culpepper, vice-president of the Ottawa-based North-South Institute, recently wrote, "History shows that countries that prosper are the most efficient traders." This may give one clue as to why Ethiopia is so poor today. The country exports only about thirty - six percent of the value of goods imported. Primary exports are coffee, leather products, and gold. Coffee— a crop subject to the vagaries of world market prices— makes up sixty percent of the total exports. (Ethiopia is one of the triumvirate of large coffee-growing nations in Africa, the others being Uganda and Cote d'Ivoire. In 1996, according to FAO statistics, Ethiopia produced 229,980 metric tons of coffee, of which 110,294 metric tons were exported.)

Despite its distressing socio-economic facts and figures, Ethiopia is making important strides forward. With an estimated GDP growth rate in 1995 and 1996 of 10.4 percent, according to World Bank figures, the country's economy was reportedly the second largest in the region after Kenya. Its 1995-1996 inflation rate—less than one percent—was the lowest in East Africa. Whereas the country had a food shortage in 1992, by 1996 it had a food surplus. Ethiopia has free access to Red Sea ports via Eritrea and the industrial and services sectors of the economy are growing. IMF- and World Bank-supported reforms have led to decontrolled prices and have allowed more private traders to enter the market.

"Whereas the rest of Africa is dropping off like leaves," Tesfaye said, "this place is coming up a bit. It has, well, frankly, grace. That's what I can say—grace. My father has confidence in this country and is investing here. In four years this government has achieved more than all other African governments combined."

Businessmen in the region, like Tesfaye and his friend Jima, are returning, rebounding, and rebuilding. Ethiopia needs men like these who believe there is a positive future in store for the country and who are willing to work hard to achieve it. Most of all, Ethiopia needs its grace.

# Bahar Dar

*One who proposes an exchange knows which is the better.*

— Ethiopian proverb

According to Ethiopian Embassy figures, Kate, Sarah, and I were three of 107,000 tourists who visited Ethiopia during 1996. The same number of people pass through the gates of Disneyland in California in just three days. Extrapolating from statistics of previous years, of the 107,000 tourists in Ethiopia in 1996, only 40,000 were from North America and Europe. For most wayfarers to Ethiopia the principal goal is to tackle what is called the Historic Route Quartet or Historic Circuit, a loop through northern Ethiopia to the towns of Bahar Dar, Gondar, Axum, and Lalibela.

Bahar Dar, on the southern shores of Lake Tana, is a pleasant town of some 54,000 people. It serves as both the embarkation point for trips to

*Julie, Kate and Sarah before the
dribbling Tisissat Falls*

Tisissat Falls on the Blue Nile, as well as for jaunts to
the thirty-seven islands in Lake Tana with their fascinating museums and monasteries, some of which are
off-limits to women. In Gondar, a city tucked into the
foothills of the Simien Mountains, one finds medieval
castles and churches and dazzling mountain scenery.
Axum, founded 2,000 years ago, is Ethiopia's oldest
city and is known for its stone *stele*, pillars carved
from single blocks of granite. The largest of these, at
ninety-eight feet (thirty meters), is the longest monolithic stone column in the world. Sometimes called
New Jerusalem, Lalibela is famous for its twelfth-
century churches built into solid rock high up in the
Lastan Mountains. We decided to loop through Bahar
Dar, Gondar, and Lalibela, leaving Axum for another
time, or perhaps another life.

Most tourists fly to Historic Route Quartet destinations. In part, they take to the skies because
Ethiopian Airlines' internal flights are inexpensive and

*Lush hotel garden in Bahar Dar*

have enjoyed a gilded reputation. The main reason, though, is because the distances are great and span rugged terrain. One would need five or six days in travel time alone to cover the circuit by road, and during the June to September rainy season roads become impassible in some areas. Consider the distances—280 miles from Addis Ababa northwest to Bahar Dar, another 90 miles around Lake Tana to Gondar, perhaps another 170 miles north to Axum, and 170 miles south to Lalibela. That's approximately 710 miles (about 1,140 kilometers), which is like driving from Washington D.C. to Chicago, mostly on dirt roads. And that doesn't even include the return trip.

\*   \*   \*

We met Jonas on the bus from the airport in Bahar Dar town. An Eritrean raised in Addis Ababa and now owner of a successful auto body repair shop in Washington, D.C., Jonas had returned to Ethiopia to

145

visit relatives and was taking a few days off from familial obligations to sightsee. We liked Jonas instantly; he proved to be a godsend.

Unbeknownst to us the "troubles" were kicking in the minute we stepped foot in Bahar Dar. While settling into our lakeside hotel, a rotund man named Said—who happened to be the owner of the bus that collects tourists from the airport—followed us to our room. He blathered on about how much the government boat costs and how much less his boat costs and how much better his trip was anyway.

"Yeah, yeah, whatever you say," Kate and I mumbled as we sorted through our things, trying to ignore this intrusion into the supposed sanctity of our hotel room.

Finding the two of us unreceptive, Said located Sarah in the garden where she was arranging with two mustachioed young men for a road trip to Tisissat Falls, or Tiss Abay as the locals call it. Said informed Sarah that we had already agreed to go with him and had settled on a price—a slippery contortion of the truth. A vigilant bargainer, Sarah asked how much.

"I already negotiated a price with your friends," he said sloughing her off.

Well, call her friends two-faced if you like, but we threw our chips in with Sarah and decided to go to Tiss Abay with the young men who organized the trip for half the price of the abrasive Said.

If anyone asks me—and they probably won't after reading this—I would place tourism in Ethiopia on a negative scale ranging from mildly irritating to a fiery inferno of travel hell. Our trip to Tisissat Falls fit solidly into the latter category.

Riding in the back of a covered pick-up truck en route to the waterfall, bouncing around like a satchel of baseballs, I found myself in a deep, introverted funk. Perhaps my mind subconsciously portended the calamity that lay ahead. I was having a hard time coming to terms with Ethiopia. It is without question a breathtakingly beautiful country. But, I found it so difficult to genuinely appreciate the beauty, to inhale it, because my breath was always being taken away by the country's callousness and horrors. Take the countryside leading toward Tiss Abay, for example. The land is heavenly blessed with fertile soil, and agricultural activity was evident. Yet, the people looked dirt poor, wore tattered clothing, and walked barefoot. Their mud and stick homes looked carelessly thrown together. The ribs of their cows poked out. And, most consequential to us, the competition for a few *birr* was beyond belief.

After a long, jarring ride the pick-up arrived at Tiss Abay village near the entrance to the falls. I call it a village, but to be more precise it was a corridor of muck framed by two rows of decrepit mud hovels mashed together like dirty marshmallows in a child's hand. And it was peopled by the most annoying beings on earth. Barefoot kids surrounded the pick-up and stared rudely at us demanding "money, pen." Several of the little monsters reached into the windows pushing our backs when they were turned and pulling our hair.

"She likes your hair," said one youngster excusing a teenage girl who had tugged on mine.

"Then why did she pull it?" I asked. "Tell her to come here. I want to pull her hair."

The teenage girl, looking mortified, covered her head with her hands and asked, "Why?"

"You pulled mine," I explained, "Now I'm going to pull yours."

The fighting in mucktown began as soon as we arrived. Local men yanked our two guides from the back of the pickup truck and started arguing viciously with them. Arms flailed in the air. Someone poked the shorter guide in the eye. That spurred a policeman, who had been standing by listlessly, into action. We never figured out exactly which camp the policeman supported, but suspected that he was the captain of his own camp playing on both sides until he netted some kind of profit. This representative of Ethiopian law enforcement chased down the eye poker, let loose a few loud slaps across his face, then hurled rocks at him after he wiggled free and sprinted away.

Now the amazing thing was that all this was taking place beside a sign that read "Ethiopian Tourist Office." A splendid howdy-do to you too! As we understood it at that stage, the hubbub stemmed from that fact that the village people claimed rights to tourists from this point on. Still reeling from thirty years of communist rule, Ethiopians had not yet adapted to free market enterprise, and these folks felt they had some sort of innate right to get a piece of the tourist pie. But we had paid for our city-slicker guides, and, particularly after this savage display on the part of the local welcoming committee, preferred to stick with them.

"He put this country back thirty years," said Jonas, referring to Mengistu and his communist regime.

"1960s?" I calculated. "No, no....we're in the dark ages here."

We managed—with Jonas constantly translating and interjecting—to move our party on its way, accompanied by the guides we had hired at our hotel. The truck stopped at the parking area for the falls and we climbed out. As our group tromped down a pathway, the locals from mucktown appeared in front of us: obviously they knew the shortcut. They attempted to pull away the skinnier of our two guides who for some reason had been singled out for their wrath.

"No, no, no," we said refusing to proceed without our guide. "He comes with us."

A community guard, an old man toting a sufficiently intimidating rifle, showed up just in time. It seemed we were free of the "terrorists," as our guides called them.

We hiked over a bridge and through the middle of a modest village clinging to a hillside where a fairly sober wedding was preoccupying all the adults. Appearing above us on the path, like a heavenly cherub, a boy strummed a *krar*, a wooden lyre. In contrast to his hypnotic presence, the small boy could only wheedle a few whiny notes out of his instrument.

*I finally make friends with the Soda Vendors*

Further along the same path, a more accomplished lad unleashed a beautiful tune from his lyre, creating a rather theatrical moment.

A few village boys, one with a hunched back and a broad grin, began to follow us. They lugged heavy bags over their shoulders, which we soon realized were filled with bottles of soda. After numerous futile attempts to shoo the pack of midget soda vendors away, I started to warm to them. After all, they were just following us and not trying to beat the daylights out of anyone, and I felt an overwhelming need to connect in some way with this strange division of humanity. I tried to explain to these up-and-coming Ethiopian entrepreneurs that tourists do not enjoy being followed literally step by step when they are seeking to view nature.

"Why don't you just plant yourself in one location," I asked, "and wait for the tourists to walk by?"

"Because," the hunchbacked one replied cleverly, "we don't know when the tourists will get thirsty."

British explorer James Bruce came upon the Tisissat Falls in 1770 during his search for the source of the 4,160-mile long Nile River. Of the falls, he wrote:

> The river had been considerably increased by the rains, and fell in one sheet of water, without any interval, about half an English mile in breadth, with a force and noise that was truly terrible, and which stunned and made me, for a time, perfectly dizzy. A thick fume or haze, covered the falls all around, and hung over the course of the stream both above and below. It was one of the most magnificent, stupendous sights in creation.

Well, the only thing we found "truly terrible" about the Tisissat Falls was the fact that we could easily have followed the path to them ourselves, without the complicating factors of guides and soft drink vendors. After all our effort, the falls were far from stupendous. We were assured that during the rainy season, when Bruce experienced them—which it wasn't, they really were impressive. One guidebook described them as a "vivid experience" with the "awesome roar of water crashing into the mist-shrouded gorge far below." There was no doubt that the experience had been vivid. But the main stream of the falls was no more than a few yards wide and splashed into a rocky pool with about as much drama as a kindergarten Christmas pageant.

It was, at any rate, a lovely unspoiled setting for a few photos: one shot of the three women; one photo of Jonas and the three women; and one of the three women and the, oh, twenty or so children that we had been unsuccessful in shaking off. Meanwhile, farmers wandered past taking little notice of this strange grouping of humans. They had mouths to feed, work to do.

My breathing became labored as we walked away from the falls up a gently sloping field of cracked black earth, and I had to stop to pay homage to the altitude. A small boy stood in a distant field bellowing out operatic melodies as we all tromped over his late afternoon landscape.

Taking an alternative route back to the truck, we come upon a river. Passengers were ferried back and forth across this narrow stretch of water by *tanqua*, papyrus reed canoes propelled by two men using poles, one at the bow, the other at the stern. The four of us and our two guides scrambled down the river bank and loaded into one of these canoes. Each of us sat with legs outstretched, wrapped around the passenger in front. River water seeped into the boat, dampening the seat of our pants. It was all very scenic and quintessentially African—that is, until quintessential Ethiopia got in the way.

Once situated, the wisenheimer boat people took that particular moment to inform us that it would cost thirty *birr* each for passage. Now, thirty *birr* was only about four dollars, but locals do not pay even one *birr* for this same ride. We all were hip to inflated prices for foreigners, but thirty times higher than the native cost was insupportable. As had been the theme throughout the day, it became a matter of principle. After much arguing, the boatmen dropped their price to twenty *birr*, which was still outrageous. So we disembarked en masse and informed the crew, as well as the two dozen people sitting along the shore, all of whom had been vocally casting their ballots in favor of the boat people, that we would turn on our heels and walk back from whence we came.

Finally, the boat crew and the shore-side audience agreed to ten each for the *ferenji* and five for Jonas since he spoke Amharic. Jonas handed over forty *birr* and the boatman refused to give him his change. One friggin' thing after another. Jonas badgered him until the change was produced, while the *ferenji* women railed at the onlookers, telling them that their mean-spirited approach would not inspire tourism. As dusk descended on the water, we floated away.

The view from the papyrus boat was blissful, and the ride along this tributary of the mighty Nile would have been nothing short of stupendous if we weren't so busy muttering about Tiss Abay's horrible people. The odd thing was, throughout the entire ruckus we never feared for our physical safety, although we had been mortally terrified for the welfare of our bony guide. We neither worried about being robbed, which can be a nagging concern in several other parts of Africa, nor about being dumped out of the boat and left to float downstream. In fact, I was amazed that our guides had left their vehicle unattended with all those "terrorists" lurking about. Jonas explained that if the villagers damaged the car they would experience real trouble. It seemed a strange set of priorities; beating the pulp out of a man was okay, but don't dare damage his stuff.

Oh, what a surprise. The terrorists were waiting for us on the other side of the river and once again they singled out skinny. We formed a circle around our guide to prevent his being dragged off and pummeled. I was reminded that the really funny thing about all this, although nobody was laughing, was that the path to the falls was so obvious that you didn't even need a guide. Maybe one less guide wouldn't have been such a bad idea after all.

Night was descending by the time we arrived back at the ramshackle village of Tiss Abay. Just when we thought the day's harassment was over, a new character jumped into the back of the truck and began arguing forcefully with Jonas. He wanted Jonas to give him a fifty *birr* (seven dollar) fee for the use of his video camera during our tour. As usual, the policeman, the terrorists, and everyone else within earshot tried to get involved.

"What does this guy want?" Kate asked.

"Who is he?" asked Sarah.

We were confused and angry. The conversation took place in Amharic. This man was particularly objectionable, and, as it turned out, was the official from the Tourist Office.

"Let's just go," I ordered the driver.

The situation, as we came to understand it, was this: under the previous regime, tourism in Ethiopia was state-controlled. Visitors were required to travel with government-assigned guides to predetermined sites. Now that Ethiopia espoused free market enterprise, locals had been given their first opportunity to get in on the tourist act. Said, the bus owner, held some sort of Mafia-like monopoly on privately run tourism in Bahar Dar and its environs. Vexed that we had chosen another operator over him for the trip to the Tisissat Falls, Said had phoned ahead from the hotel (a hotel worker later informed us) to the Tourist Office in Tiss Abay village and promised—we assumed—cash incentives to the villagers to rough up our guides.

Not only did we find Said despicable, but, as the picture became clearer, we became annoyed that our guides had used us and our vacation time to engage in union busting. We also learned that the troublemakers at Tisissat Falls, in particular the policeman and the pest from the Tourist Office, had previously served six months in jail for similar antagonistic activities.

We should have suspected foul play when we checked into our hotel. The elderly, bespectacled manager initially charged us 150 *birr* each, but Said, so magnanimous with other people's profits, scolded him for overcharging and brought the price down to 100 *birr* each. The manager then leaned against a counter and looked at us.

"Is anyone going to check us in?" I asked.

"We all have different jobs here," he said, as his reception desk remained unmanned. "Everyone has his own specialty."

His specialty, Sarah noted, appeared to be bad management.

Nighttime in Bahar Dar was clement and rendered a welcome respite from the continual hounding of the long, hot day. Dim street lamps lit a wide, palm-tree-lined main road. Sweet smelling jasmine perfumed the air, while bats squeaked overhead. We could hear the deep sound of drums and the faint cacophony of a wedding celebration in the distance.

As usual in Ethiopia, the most destitute of the destitute lay asleep under rags along the concrete walls surrounding the church. One of these beings sat upright under a cloth. Even though it was covered, his pointy-head eerily followed our gaze as we walked past. From the ledge of the church's high wall a glittering object peered down at me: I couldn't make out whether it was a gilded religious statue mocking the poor reclining below or a stone-faced beggar staring out into the night.

"This was once a famous place," Jonas reminisced. "This whole country was one of the best in Africa. So beautiful!"

I asked Jonas if he'd like to move back to Ethiopia one day.

"When I left it was good," he replied, "now it's bad. The people...well, you saw them. Why should I come back?"

# Lake Tana

*When a wise man is foolish, it is a big matter.*

— Ethiopian proverb

"How can they have water problems?" Kate snarled first thing in the morning. "They have a whole fucking lake!"

We called for the hotel repairman to find out why there was no water pressure in our bathroom.

"The gardener is watering the lawn," said Kate, presenting probable cause.

Ignoring her comment, the repairman began banging on pipes and flipping knobs, while the hotel manager and other staff tramped back and forth through our room discussing the problem with each other in Amharic.

The water gushed out of the pipes, miraculously, when the gardener turned off the hose. The repairman sat on the edge of the bathtub for a good five minutes afterward alternating glancing down at the running water and then looking into the room at us.

Jonas arrived in time to translate: "He wants to show you that it's working."

"Okay, thank you," said Kate for the tenth time, only this time much louder.

The repairman shuffled out of the room. Good morning Ethiopia.

Any day, anywhere improves with breakfast al fresco. Lavender jacaranda petals fluttered onto our metal table. The hotel grounds came alive with the chirping of birds. Rays of sun filtered through the flower garden making it a medley of color: saffron marigolds, crimson poinsettias, magenta bougainvillaea bushes, and butter and cream flowers atop frangipani trees with their crooked branches beckoning skyward. A fig tree with a massive trunk drooped its green branches over the lake's edge.

Curiously, the waiters kept taking away our drinks before we had finished them, and on several occasions it looked as if a waiter would miss the table when setting down our coffee cups. One porter who tried to close the zipper on Sarah's backpack before carrying it for her had an inordinate amount of trouble finding the pull tab. Sarah pointed out the unusual fact that all the waiters and porters wore the same style of eye-glasses: that is, thick black frames and Coke-bottle lenses. I had heard stories about second-hand prescription glasses being sent to Africa where patients try on different pairs until they find a reasonable match. Perhaps this happened in Bahar Dar.

We decided to take no chances with private enterprise that day and walked straight to the government boat dock. The ticket seller was nowhere to be found. One worker told us to come back after lunch. It was 9:30 in the morning. We saw several men sitting under the shade of an umbrella at the lakeside cafe sipping espressos and silently observing the scene. Jonas was persistent, telling every person he saw to find the ticket taker. We wanted to pay exorbitant prices for a government boat, now!

After the group of espresso-slurping men left, we learned that they, in fact, were the dock administrators—the ones who were supposed to be running the place. According to Jonas, this was their version of passive resistance against Ethiopia's Tigray-run government. We were in Amhara country now. The name Amhara derives from Hebrew and means "mountain people." The Amharas ruled Ethiopia for centuries and had not yet come to terms with their precipitous fall from power. From what I could tell, many Amharas were bitter about the loss of Eritrea, but they were even more bitter about their loss of control in Ethiopia, which they had dominated for the better part of the last five hundred years. *Amara yazzal inji ayatazzezim,* says an Amhara proverb: The Amhara are to rule, not to be ruled.

It was in AD 1270 that an Amharic nobleman Yekuno Amlak declared himself ruler of the Christian Kingdom of Ethiopia. He based his claim to kingship on his descendancy from the biblical union of Solomon and Sheba. All succeeding monarchs of Ethiopia have traced their ancestry to Yekuno Amlak and thus to this same claim of legitimacy. For the past several decades, under the Mengistu regime, the Amharas continued to hold sway over Ethiopia, although under an entirely different political structure. Mengistu spoke a good game about wiping out the last vestiges of imperial rule, particularly those based on ethnic and class privilege, but Amharic dominance persisted, this time along the lines of cultural imperialism. Under Mengistu's watch, Amharic became the official language of government, education, news sources, and commerce. Amharas became landholders and were dispatched throughout the country as government administrators. Today, Ethiopians live under a government directed largely by Tigrayans, a predominantly Christian people of the northern highlands who compose some twelve to fifteen percent of Ethiopia's population. Many Amharas view the current Tigray-run government as tribalistic and biased toward the northern regions of the country.

During the Mengistu era, explained Jonas, people who were opposed to the government would not have

*A payprus reed canoe to cross the Blue Nile*

dared, for fear of retribution, a work "go-slow" like we were experiencing at the docks. But under the new, more tolerant government, these men could afford to express their discontent by simply relaxing.

While we waited for the ticket man, a waiter grabbed a key and proudly led Sarah and me to the newly constructed toilets.

En route, the waiter asked me, "Where from?"

I was not on my guard so early in the day. "America," I replied gaily.

"I-you-take-address, because I don't have sponsor."

Quickly snapping back into Ethiopia survival mode, I said to the waiter, "I am not about to sponsor someone who I have met for only one minute."

Apparently my tone was strong enough, because even though he probably could not understand the words, he got my drift and piped down. The brand new toilets were foul. The bowls were blocked up with human waste, and zillions of mosquitoes had taken up residence in the room. Sarah and I waited until the waiter left and jumped down behind a wall to squat among the trees.

The pair of tour guides from the previous day had shown up at our hotel in the morning and trailed us to the government docks. They waited around for the hour or so it took us to organize the trip. As the boat pulled away from the dock, the denser of the two jumped on board with us. I knew how to play their game by then.

"You must pay 100 *birr* to join us," I said.

"No, no." He shook his head. "I don't cost you any more."

"No." I shook my head. "If you want to come, you must contribute to the cost of hiring the boat."

He leapt back onto the dock and the two guides stood looking forlorn as the boat chugged out into the lake.

The government boat was a large piecemeal job. The bottom half was painted sky blue, the top half white, like government-regulated taxis, but this vessel had the lovely addition of a rusty red deck. A large Ethiopian flag with its red, green, and gold bands flapped off the stern. Lake Tana is a huge expanse of murky water covering 1,429 square miles (3,700 square kilometers), making it bigger than the state of Rhode Island. As James Bruce discovered in 1770, the lake is the source of the Blue Nile.

A Pied Kingfisher perched like a beacon on top of a tree beside the lake. Ducks flew in and took rides on the boat's wake. Cormorants fished, their serpentine necks wiggling out of the water then plunging down again. They looked like miniature Loch Ness monsters. One cormorant dried its outstretched wings on a rock, while a vulture perched on another rock nearby. The top of a lakeside tree was covered with marabou storks that, from a distance, resembled enormous gnarled blossoms.

We arrived at the first of the sacred islands of Lake Tana unsure of what to expect and walked single file inland through a forest. Black monkeys with hairy white faces scampered alongside us keeping a safe distance from the narrow path. Hoards of children tagged along, like a mobile market place, displaying old silver crosses strung on pieces of yarn, colorful hand-woven baskets, Haile Selassie coin necklaces, religious paintings on cured animal skins, and religious icons. The answer to the question, "Who made this?" was inevitably, "My father." As might be expected, the children were overly aggressive in their sales tactics.

The first church we visited was surrounded by a high stone wall. We entered through an earthen and reed gatehouse. Before us stood the largest mud hut any of us had ever seen. The hut's roof was high and conical and had been impeccably thatched.

"Great," I muttered to myself, having difficulty containing my petulance, "We've come all this way to see

*A monk/priest at an island church/monastery
in Lake Tana, Ethiopia*

a damnable big mud hut!" We walked closer. A decrepit priest swung open massive doors hewn from solid slabs of wood, releasing a waft of cool air that brushed past our skin and snapped me out of my contrariness. As our eyes adjusted, we saw brilliant hues peeping out from the dark interior. Paintings covered every inch of the inner walls, as well as the wooden ceiling beams. Dating from the twelfth and thirteenth centuries, the paintings tell stories of saints and of Jesus and Mary. These fabulous works of art were as refreshing as the cool breeze.

Several Ethiopian tourists shared the fact that preparing the durable paint used on the old paintings was such a complicated process that it took three years. We used flashlights and the light on Jonas's video camera to view some of the paintings, which are preserved in total darkness. Worn-out curtains protected the more frail sections of these works. In one church we later visited, brand new long flowery curtains covered most of the walls; the priest explained that a tourist had seen the previous dusty, torn old curtains and sent these new ones as a gift.

At another church, standing in front of a low, broad stone wall, a bucktoothed wise man shared one of the island's legends. Long ago, said the impromptu storyteller, when the priests were building this wall around the church, there was one boulder so huge that none of the priests could move it. Hot and tired, the priests decided to break for lunch. When they returned, the boulder had been fitted into place. The priests could not figure out who had moved this massive boulder, until one priest spotted a hoof print in a nearby rock. They knew then that the boulder had been carried to the wall by a magical horse. At this juncture, the storyteller pointed to an imprint in a rock that, sure as I'm alive, looked like a horse's hoof print.

The island's museum was also housed in a mud hut, although much smaller than the churches. The caretaker, a gaunt old man with a toothy grin, opened the wooden door of the museum with a key. Watching him through the doorway, we saw him then unlock an interior door. He descended a few steps, unlocked another door, descended a few more steps, and opened yet another door, and another. It looked as though he was plunging right into the earth's core.

When the museum keeper ascended from the bowels of the hut, he carried glittering silver crowns, an old velvet cape hung with silver baubles, and an ancient handpainted book. He arranged these items on a wooden table inside the hut and then swung open a pair of shutters so that those of us standing outside could view the treasures. He told us that the pieces formerly belonged to Ethiopian kings and queens who donated them to the monastery.

A rather unique concept, I thought, requiring tourists to make the considerable effort of coming to the place where the objects originated rather than having the pieces gathered up and locked in an urban museum. Whether electronic security devices at metropolitan museums are more efficient than the subterranean security systems of these island museums I do not know, but decentralized museums in Podunk towns probably do make theft more tempting for amateurs. We heard that a German tourist had recently been caught trying to steal historic treasures from Axum.

For religious reasons, the monks living on these islands are not allowed to cultivate the land and can only eat what grows naturally. The islands' wild plants included coffee, hops, and lemons. Standing beside the museum, I picked up a lemon that had fallen from a tree and received the okay sign from the monks to indulge. I tore the fruit open and squeezed refreshing lemon drops into everyone's parched mouths. When I finally squeezed some of the tart juice into my own mouth my throat muscles clamped together like a vise-grip and I couldn't breath. I clutched Kate's shoulder, bent over, and gasped for air. Meanwhile, the others stood by wide-eyed and scared witless, aware that no medical facilities are on the island and that getting back to Bahar Dar would take several hours. It was difficult for them not to imagine the worst. Inclined toward asthma, I knew that if I could just relax, eventually my breathing would return. It was only a matter of minutes before I was breathing normally again, but it seemed interminable.

"I'm glad you are still with us," Jonas said repeatedly as we walked down the path back to the boat. Jonas later relayed this story to his family in Addis. His relatives concluded that I stopped breathing because food growing on that island was sacred and was meant only for the monks.

By the time we reached the dock, the sales children had resorted to standard lines of desperation:

"Pen, pen, pen."

"Something for me."

"Something to remember you by."

One boy handed me a "business card" cut from a cardboard box.

"I am an adult," I scolded the boy. "I don't have time to write to children."

He retrieved the card and returned it to his stack of cards, no doubt reserving it for the next, more compliant, tourist.

Back on the boat, the astute crewmen had iced down soft drinks and beers to sell to their passengers. We imbibed and happily paid the moderately inflated prices in support of legitimate ways of acquiring tourist dollars. We basked under the sharp highland sun, the wind tousling our hair, and daydreamed about the potential of this romantic lake. A true American capitalist, I imagined lakeside resorts and water skiing.

"That would be a shame," said Sarah reflecting her PC British side.

"They need the tourist money," noted Kate, a Canadian pragmatist.

"I'd like to set up houseboat tours," mused Jonas, the Eritrean, gone American.

\* \* \*

The previous day, I had serious reservations about why I subjected myself to the frustrations of Africa.

165

What on earth was an American woman in her mid-thirties doing bouncing around in the back of a rickety pick-up truck, driving through wretched villages, fending off shuckers? By the evening of the second day in Bahar Dar, I knew why. Our day cruising around Lake Tana had been splendid, and after showers, we were all feeling fabulous.

Jonas, Sarah, Kate, and I strolled into the poorly lit sidestreets of Bahar Dar. The few streetlights that had been functioning snapped off, and the night was suddenly as black and still as sleep. We stopped walking and took advantage of the moment to examine the stars blanketing the sky, patiently waiting for the lights to return, as we knew they would. It was Saturday night in Bahar Dar, and if one didn't know better they would think the town had been torched in an afternoon raid and the doused fires were still smoldering. No, this London-style fog was the simple product of hundreds of charcoal stoves on which coffee beans roasted and frankincense burned.

Dirt roads blended into earthen houses. Attendants sat in tiny shops with crooked frames, shelves jammed with essentials, resting on their elbows in the warm yellow light of kerosene lanterns. Bars were ubiquitous. Their interior walls were painted in bright pinks, reds, and purples that contrasted with the night sky. Several of these watering holes tried to lure customers with foil-wrapped shelves and colorful strands of twinkly lights. Although the shelves looked well stocked with liquor bottles, none of the bars, at this hour, had any patrons.

We ate dinner at *Enkutatash* ("New Year" in Amharic), a delightful restaurant where tables and chairs were crammed into colorful rooms. The place was clean, the waiters efficient, and the stereo speakers in miraculously good condition. As was common in many parts of rural Africa, they played country music.

"Do you feel at home, Julie?" Sarah teased.

I did feel at home when we saw a group of boys crowded around a foosball table, although this one was not in a college bar but casually set out in the

*Jonas, Julie, and Sarah celebrate the end of a
long day in Bahar Dar*

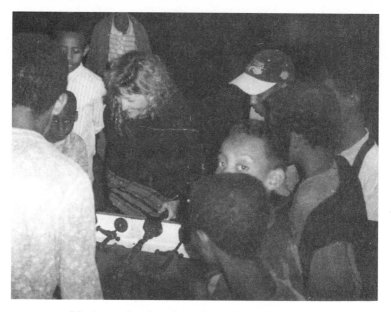

*My team is victorious in street-side foosball*

street. The foosball men were so worn and blackened that you could no longer make out the team colors. Jonas and I entered the foosball fray, each joining opposing teams. My partner took the defensive position away from me.

"Because," the young man explained, "you don't know how to play."

"How do you know?" I said, and, with a snap of my wrist, proceeded to score the first two points.

Each point earned yelps of excitement and a handshake from my partner as well as from an observer or two. Great guffaws filled the night air as our team solidly defeated Jonas's.

We capped off the evening sipping beers beside the lake. The night air was blessedly cool. Chirping crickets supplied soothing background noise, while soft voices punctuated the night. Africa does this to you. One day it puts you through great stress, the next day it pampers you. Africa makes your life hellish, only to turn around and present you with a glimpse of heaven. With its chaos and frustrations, it throws you into a blind rage, then—like the island churches of Lake Tana—amazes you with incredible achievements against all odds. Africa reaches untapped emotions and then stretches them to the limits; that is the precise reason people say they feel more alive in Africa.

# Gondar

*Who hits the father, hits the son.*

— Ethiopian proverb

We had barely sucked in one breath of the air in Gondar when, to use a crude America expression, the shit hit the fan. As Sarah, Kate, and I exited the airport several taxi drivers approached us. Logically, we chose the one who quoted the lowest fare. We walked la-la-la to the cab and started loading our bags onto the roof rack. Another taxi driver appeared and the two cabbies began arguing. The heated discussion quickly escalated into a shoving match, then a tug-of-war over Kate's backpack. The three of us just stared at them.

"We are completely irrelevant in this game," Sarah observed.

Jonas, whose Gondar relatives had picked him up at the airport, climbed out of his family's car to come, once again, to the aid of his three girlfriends.

"Tell them it's our fare," we groaned. "We have the right to decide which taxi we will use."

Once again we were reminded that Ethiopians hadn't fully grasped the concept of free enterprise. They still used the old totalitarian might means right method. A policeman was called over to arbitrate the dispute. He was a scrawny man and completely ineffectual, so he decided to lead the fighting cabbies away for mediation by a superior officer.

"Oh, no you don't," we said. "Now you are wasting our time." We adopted Ethiopian taxi-driver behavior ourselves and piled into the taxi.

"Let's go. Now!" we commanded.

Throughout the hubbub a group of four Ethiopians sat inside the other taxi without saying a word: such an odd juxtaposition of aggression and what one travel book called an "inordinately polite" populace.

The victorious cabdriver was named Zelalem Fesseha, which he said means "always happy." Zelalem had mahogany-skin, a belly shaped like a baby's head, and sat as straight as a silver cross in the driver's seat, gripping the wheel at the ten o'clock and two o'clock position.

"It's not a taxi, it's a Landcruiser!" he shouted as we sped through a small village, dodging potholes and nearly clipping pedestrians. "Sometimes I taxi driver, sometimes I king!" Zelalem laughed heartily, honking his horn at the children and waving his long arm out the window.

"Well, tomorrow," I asked, "are you a taxi driver or a king? Because Kate needs a ride to the airport."

We deposited our bags at our hilltop hotel and rushed down a windy goat path leading to town. Kate had only one afternoon in Gondar before she split off from us to take a quick swing through Lalibela before returning to Nairobi. Our destination was the Debre Birhan Selassie Church with its famed painted ceiling. We inquired after the church's whereabouts with two men sitting on a bridge at the bottom of the hill. The men directed us up a road that led into a small forest.

*In Ethiopia, you'll never be lonely.*

We were followed incessantly by people of all ages calling out "you, you, you" and asking the standard questions:

"What's your country?"

"What's your name?"

"What's your job?"

"Where you go?"

A few locals managed to eke out a most appreciated, "Welcome to Ethiopia."

In the 1960s, travel guide writer Robert S. Kane painted a more congenial picture of Ethiopia's citizenry. In his book *Africa A to Z*, Kane observed "good-natured children anxious to greet strangers to their town with wide, infectious grins." But, for two decades of communist rule, from the mid-1970s through 1991, tourism was tightly controlled in Ethiopia. Leaving Addis required a permit and tourists were restricted to government hotels. The northern reaches of the country, including Axum and Lalibela, were off-limits because of rebel activity in the region.

Because we knew this, Sarah, Kate and I extended the locals of Gondar the benefit of the doubt. We discussed the fact that the people might be unaware of how their actions would be viewed as discourteous in other cultures. Our conversation went like this:

"They don't know how abrasive 'you, you, you' sounds."

"They don't realize tourists are asked the same set of questions by every kid in Ethiopia and that we are tired of answering them."

"They don't realize we want to be left alone."

"They just want to talk to us."

"We are walking right through the middle of their neighborhoods."

On the other hand, it was pretty darned obvious we were annoyed. I felt fairly confident that rudeness was not a culturally acceptable trait in Ethiopia. But adults rarely attempted to curtail irksome behavior and even engaged in it themselves on occasion. Perhaps the adults had abdicated responsibility, aware that these unruly youth were taking over their land. Coming into this decade, over fifty percent of the Ethiopian population was under fifteen years old.

The forest road came to a dead end at a noisy power station guarded by a snarling dog. Something was fishy. It wouldn't be the first time in Eritrea and Ethiopia that we had been completely led astray—and of course, there were no signposts. We retraced our steps over the long route back to town and marched up an entirely different steep road.

Finally, on a hill northeast of the city, we located Debre Birhan Selassie; a stone and thatch church built in the 1670s during the rule of Iyasu the Great. Once inside, we all collapsed onto the floor from heat and exhaustion—an ideal vantage point for admiring the painted ceiling with its rows of angel faces, their wide brown eyes staring off in different directions.

The caretaker, standing nearby in a white robe and white skullcap, allowed us to rest, gawk, and take photographs. A beam of sunlight streamed through the opening of the bulky wooden door. The walls were covered with biblical scenes, although more faded than the paintings in the island churches of Lake Tana. Saint George was slaying the dragon, as he does in many of Ethiopia's religious sites. The majority of characters in these paintings, such as saints and angels, are depicted as Ethiopian. Interestingly, warriors' faces are always shown full on, while enemy faces are in profile.

Viewing Debre Birhan Selassie lifted our spirits. We gained the presence of mind to be able to joke with Ethiopia's children and even stopped to watch boys playing marbles in a patch of dirt beside the road. A herd of cattle, with no apparent owner, ambled toward town, lumbered down broad concrete steps, and drifted into the middle of a downtown street. Meanwhile, several sheep slept in a grassy median strip on another busy road. No one seemed to notice but us.

Walking up one street, we saw a group of kids beating the pulp out of each other, as we had learned Ethiopians are prone to do. Some adults came over and we expected them to break up the scuffle, but instead they threw a few punches themselves.

"God, this is really primeval," Sarah blurted out.

Again we tried to force perspective. We imagined Ethiopians watching a Canadian ice hockey match or a Hollywood action movie. Would our cultures also appear senselessly violent?

We were fortunate, I suppose, to be in Ethiopia in the 1990s, and not the 1970s. At that time, Ryszard Kapuscinski reported:

> Their thoughts run not toward life but toward death. At first they talk quietly, then a quarrel breaks out, and the dispute ends in gunfire. Where do so much stubbornness, aggression, and hatred come from? All this without a moment's thought, without brakes, rolling over the edge of a cliff.

We hoped that what was different about the 1990s was that Ethiopians would stop short of the cliff.

Either Gondarines had an unusually gay sense of color, or certain paints were more readily available and inexpensive than others. One store was half shocking pink, the other half gold. Another building had an aqua second floor and violet ground floor, highlighted by blood-red windows and doors. Interiors communicated the Ethiopian penchant for half-and-half style too, like the bar we stopped into for a much-needed Pepsi where the walls were painted part pastel pink and part sky blue. We were served by three grinning girls, the youngest of whose head barely poked above the bar, and the oldest no more than twelve years old. We saw no one else around.

Next stop, Ethiopia Hotel for real sustenance. Situated on a bustling corner of town, this was a popular bar. We were the only female patrons. This simple observation reminded me that no matter how free Sarah, Kate, and I are as Western women to travel and explore the length and breadth of our planet, there are still plenty of women in this world who wouldn't even dream of entering the corner bar for a drink.

Ethiopia took on a whole new air after a couple of cold beers. In our light-headed state, we boldly joked with—or rather at—local inquisitors, much to their confusion.

The government-owned Goha Hotel, where we were staying, is perched on the crest of a hill overlooking the ancient city and the surrounding jagged terrain. Sunset was the ideal time to soak in the hotel's magnificent panoramic view of crisscrossing peaks and valleys. The three of us stood on the edge of the bluff, our hair fluttering in the wind, while above us kites and pied crows soared on the updrafts of the early evening breeze. One kite dive-bombed an Ethiopian guest's head, trying to snatch his blue baseball cap.

The sun, a radiant orb tumbling behind the mountains, transformed the city's pastel buildings in the valley below into gemstones glowing in firelight. We could see a medieval castle in the distance and counted three minarets.

The muezzin's sundown call to prayer was overpowered by reggae music pounding out of a boombox nearby. Its owner looked an awful lot like a returnee. He was dressed in blue jean overalls, wore drug-dealer sunglasses, and chain-smoked cigarettes. A waiter carried his boombox for him, high up on his shoulder, as if it was chilled champagne on a silver tray. The man, in the meantime, found himself a seat beside the pool. Another waiter appeared with a single beer on a tray, also held exaggeratedly high, like some sort of poorly choreographed beer commercial. The other guests chuckled at the scene: the man may have become "westernized," but he certainly did not share a westerner's concept of what a peaceful drink at sunset should be like.

Kate departed early in the morning, carried away before we opened our eyes in King Zelalem Fesseha's royal chariot. Later, Sarah and I, feeling suddenly lonely for her company scrambled down the goat path toward town where we met up with Jonas. Jonas's uncle owns the Simien supermarket located in the heart of Gondar near the piazza, a small square over-powered by the Art Deco-style telecommunications building that Sarah dubbed the "in your face build-ing." His uncle once owned the entire city block, according to Jonas, but the property was confiscated during the Mengistu regime. The uncle had calculated that land and buildings were a wise and sober invest-ment for the future. In hindsight, he realized that his family would have been just as well off today had he lavished their money on more fleeting luxuries.

The Simien supermarket could have been a depres-sion-era general store in America. The cash register and radio may have been issued about that time. Under large glass counters toiletries, sweets, and other miscellany were displayed. Wooden shelves reached to the ceiling loaded with canned and packaged goods. Townspeople dropped in clutching a few wrinkled *birr* notes in their hands, looking for bits and pieces. The clerk weighed bulk items on a beautifully preserved antique Italian scale. Two shy boys held out a few coins in their palms and requested a special type of *mastika*, chewing gum. A couple of young men exam-ined lengths of electrical wire.

The store was tended by the owner's daughter Melitte, an amber-skinned beauty who had recently returned from India where she earned a master's degree in economics. While listening intently to our horror stories of Bahar Dar, she showed a customer a tin of pineapple spears and then returned the can to the shelf. She carefully rotated the label forward to keep it in line with the other cans.

Melitte warmly greeted a handsome young man who entered the store, kissing him on both cheeks. He asked me how I liked Ethiopia.

"Addis is shocking," I replied.

Everyone in the shop agreed. These are small town folk, who like small town folk everywhere shake their heads and say tsik-tsik at the thought of the big city, the modern Sodom and Gomorrah. Melitte proceeded to retell the story of our experiences in Bahar Dar, rattling off words faster than I had ever heard anyone speak before and employing copious hand motions.

The young man shook his head and commiserated, saying, "Sorry, sorry. Sorry for that." Then he asked, "Well, how do you like Gondar?"

"It's very nice," I replied.

Both Melitte and her friend chimed, "Thank you, thank you!" as if I had complimented them on their first-born child.

Jonas, Sarah, and I made a day of exploring Gondar's medieval castles and its market along cobbled streets. Legend has it that Gondar's royal status came into being because an archangel appeared to Emperor Lebna Dengel in a dream, revealing that Ethiopia's sacred capital would be found in a place beginning with the letter *g*. Emperors who followed Lebna Dengel searched for this mystical site. But, it wasn't found until the early 1600s, when Emperor Fasilades was drinking from a lake, looked up and saw a holy man rising from the water. The holy man told Fasilades that he was standing in the paradise of Ezra and Enoch, and that he should build his capital on the spot, which happened to be called Gondar. Gondar remained the capital of Ethiopia for over two hundred years, from Fasilades' reign in 1632 until Emperor Tewodros fell from power in 1868.

Resident Portuguese may have influenced the design of Gondar's stone castles and palaces, but our guide was quick to point out that Axumite influences were identifiable as well. The rooms were no longer filled with ornate rugs and baroque furniture or closed off by bulky doors and windows; they were just rock walls and crumbling mortar. With a good imagination, one could envision the eloquent receptions held for dignitaries in entry rooms, sumptuous feasts in cavernous dining halls, and the certain cruelties being meted out somewhere in dank chambers down below. The highest floors of the castles provided commanding views of the hills surrounding Gondar. The palace grounds were brittle and well trodden. The most exciting feature for me was the mere fact that there are locally built medieval castles in Africa—an unusual sight indeed.

Jonas's relatives invited Sarah and me to dinner at their house around the corner from the supermarket. Inside, the concrete living room walls were painted aqua. Pillows with embroidered slipcovers were neatly arranged on the couches and chairs. Formal portraits of family members hung high up on the walls. Positioning photos and paintings close to the ceiling was one of those curious African traits that I have never understood, have never asked about, and have never devised a theory for. I just accept it as an African quirk.

We had looked forward all day to home-cooked Ethiopian food. Likewise, Jonas's aunt had spent the day anticipating the arrival of his guests at her house. To suit our Western tastes, she prepared heaps of spaghetti with meat sauce. Sarah and I glanced at one another and, masking our disappointment, ate as much as we possibly could. But it was not enough for the aunt, who became angry when she saw the large amount of pasta remaining on the coffee table. She dismissed our protests with a disgusted wave of her hand and turned back to the kitchen where she continued to oversee more cooking, no doubt with the aid of a domestic helper.

At ten o'clock, Jonas's uncle and Melitte returned home accompanied by several of the store clerks. The uncle wore thick glasses and revealed an easy smile. Elderly and moving slowly, he still appeared strong. Jonas's family was fortunate enough to own one of the estimated 100,000 television sets in Ethiopia. The father switched on the television and became absorbed in the latest news about the trials of 5,198 Ethiopians charged with genocide and war crimes under the previous regime. The family scene—everyone gathered around the television, the husband arriving home late from work and bringing young clerks with him, a mother irritated because her guests didn't eat enough, helpful daughters, modest but meticulously kept furnishings—was uncannily reminiscent of the summer of 1976 that I spent living with a family in northern Italy.

Jonas told us they expected that many of Mengistu's accomplices would receive the death penalty. While his colleagues face death sentences in Ethiopia, the fifty-year-old Mengistu lives in exile in Zimbabwe. However, he is such an outcast there, our hosts claimed, that he can't even leave his compound. Jonas's uncle expressed dismay at the Sudan's refusal to turn over Egyptian President Mubarak's would-be assassins to authorities in Ethiopia where the assassination attempt had taken place.

There was one television station in Ethiopia and it broadcast for only a few hours each evening. Much of this airtime was consumed by the news shown in three different languages—Amharic, Tigrinya, and Oromo. These were only three of the 286 languages spoken in the country. The complexities of multilingual societies must surely be one of the factors dragging down Africa's growth in the field of communications, particularly the areas of broadcasting and literature. Sarah and I couldn't understand any of Ethiopia's broadcast languages, but when the camera pointed to items spread out on the ground—television sets, radios, knives, guns—it became clear that we were watching a story about the Ethiopian police apprehending thieves. The camera slowly panned the faces of the offenders. It seems that public humiliation plays a role in crime prevention in Ethiopian society.

From 1946 to 1960, Ethiopian police officers trained under Swedish instructors at the Ethiopian Police College at Sendafa near Addis Ababa. Even today, the police are credited with northern European efficiency. A resident of Addis Ababa talked about a case in which a hijacked car was returned to the owner within a few hours. Security may come at a price, however. There have been reports of police brutalizing, and even killing, criminal suspects.

Yes, there was a certain sense of security in Ethiopia, but for me it didn't stem from the knowledge that there are efficient, armed policemen running around; rather it came from knowing there were people like Jonas and his relatives who were willing to bend over backwards to look out for us.

# Lalibela

*It is easy to become a monk in one's old age.*

— Ethiopian proverb

Ethiopian Airlines was operated and maintained by TWA when John Gunther wrote *Inside Africa* in the 1950s. It was, in Gunther's estimation, "one of the most remarkable airlines in the world." Referring to their internal flights, Gunther called it a "hop-skip-jump airline" and noted that it "hops, skips, and jumps on time." Ethiopian Airlines in the 1990s is a hurry-up-and-wait airline.

Arriving at the Gondar airport by sunrise, Sarah and I were bumped off our flight to Lalibela in favor of a large, loud group of Italian tourists. An airport attendant informed us that the next plane to Lalibela departed at 9:00 a.m. A reasonable two-hour wait Sarah and I agreed, easily slipping into African time. We had heard of incidences of flights departing *earlier* than scheduled, so initially we counted ourselves among the lucky.

The next official we talked to, however, said the plane was leaving at 10:00 a.m. We began to get suspicious. The unfortunate airport worker who told us the flight was not leaving at 10:00 a.m., but 10:30 a.m., got caught in the crossfire of our fury. To appease us, the airline sprang for a breakfast of egg sandwiches and orange juice at the airport cafe. The manager walked up to our table.

"Are we forgiven?" he demanded.

Somehow, his tone didn't bode well for the experiences that lay ahead.

Ethiopia was on high alert during our trip. Frequently, bank and hotel customers were searched, and on several occasions we were asked to leave our cameras at guards stations. And for good reason. Not long before our arrival, the Ghion Hotel in Addis Ababa was bombed and several weeks later another government hotel, the Ras in Dire Dawa, suffered a similar fate. The discovery of a body in the rubble at the Ras Hotel sparked rumors that the bomber blew himself up. Later, an ethnic Somali separatist movement Al Itahad claimed responsibility for both attacks as well as for an assassination attempt on a high-level government official.

During check-in at one airport, the security staff were so pedantic that they removed everything from passenger hand luggage that remotely resembled a weapon—tubes of lotion, spray perfumes, matches, my Walkman headphones—and made passengers transfer these hazardous items to their checked luggage.

Our frustrating experiences with internal flights led Sarah and I to the conclusion that tight security on Ethiopian Airlines was not, in fact, to prevent the odd disgruntled Ethiopian from hijacking a plane to the Sudan. It was the exasperated tourist they were really worried about: "Take me back to Addis today," screams the crazed tourist waving a tube of petroleum jelly in the pilot's face, "or else!"

A commentary in Ethiopia's *Monitor* newspaper, written two years later, touched on the same concept. The story read:

> At the airport at Axum the writer of this article witnessed old Japanese ladies ordered to remove their shoes for security check up. Was there a possibility at all that these ladies would highjack the aircraft to Europe, perhaps? But didn't they come via Europe?

Once aboard the flight to Lalibela, we quickly forgot our airport woes, sat back, and enjoyed the ride. The Twin Otter flew low enough to give a bird's eye view of the thrilling scenery of northern Ethiopia, characterized by rugged mountains, isolated plateaus, and twisting gorges. According to Philip M. Allen and Aaron Segal, in their book *The Traveler's Africa*, one traveler described Ethiopia as the Tibet of Africa. Over a century earlier, in the 1860s, a British soldier in the Napier Expedition, commented on Ethiopia's terrain, saying, "They tell us this is a table land. If it is, they have turned the table upside down and we are scrambling up and down the legs."

"It's like I imagine the Andes," Sarah exclaimed.

"Like the Grand Canyon," I said. "Without color."

Reflecting the roles we'd come to adopt on this journey, she saw up, and I saw down.

The dun-colored land below was frighteningly parched. At one-and-a-half miles high and bearing down on the equator, this part of the earth literally bakes under the sun. Snaking through canyons were rivers, once swollen wide, that were now reduced to dribble, like ribbons spread along gifts of dark soil. The scant greenery that remained clung tightly to the sides of the riverbeds. The *belg*, the short rains, were badly needed.

Villages lay high atop plateaus or snuggled in remote valleys. How on earth did the residents get there, we wondered? Moreover, how do they survive there? There were dirt tracks below. Perhaps they were roads; perhaps they were goat paths. Ethiopia has the lowest road density in Africa, and three-quarters of all farms are located at least a half day's walk to an all-weather gravel road. Certainly, many travel to their remote villages by hoof: with nearly three million horses, five million donkeys, and 630,000 mules, according to 1996 FAO statistics, the country can boast the most pack animals in Africa.

The pilot pushed open the cabin door and flashed a milk-white smile. His eyes were deep brown like those of the religious paintings, and his hair waxen-black. Descending from the small aircraft onto Lalibela's hot dusty runway, we saw that outgoing passengers were waiting in a corrugated metal departure shed, stashed there like chickens in a coup. A woman wearing a white top waved at us as if seeing long-lost friends glimpsed by chance in passing ships at sea. It was Kate, and even from that distance it was easy to discern a look of distress on her face. She was released from the shed. The three of us, briefly reunited, prattled on frantically, sharing our latest experiences and gaining Lalibela survival tips from Kate. All the while, a stern airport worker stood off to the side.

"Time is up," she informed us, her demeanor like that of a maximum-security prison guard.

Kate and Sarah glared at her and continued gabbing, but her authority effectively intimidated me. I tried to wrap up our conversation and nervously backed away.

Heavy construction machinery was present at the Lalibela airport, as we had seen in Gondar, and we were told that the government was constructing new international airports at these places. Unfathomable! Currently the flights to these remote towns carried only a couple handfuls of tourists each day. A Canadian diplomat in Addis Ababa, whom we later asked about this, scoffed.

"They don't have the infrastructure to support tourism on that scale," he commented.

Feeling completely sour on Ethiopia myself, I remarked to the diplomat that I would recommend to friends that they wait twenty years or so, until the place was more organized, before coming to see Ethiopia's exquisite historic sites.

He cringed and chuckled at the same time, saying "Organized?"

A government bus collected other tourists and us from the airport and charged an exorbitant fare for the ascent to Lalibela town, which, at an altitude of 8,524 feet (2,600 meters), was almost two miles high. As the bus snaked up precipices it rocked back and forth drawing excited chatter and titters from members of a German tour group. The Germans were loaded down with backpacks and every last one of their faces was sunburnt. Chugging along a windy, craggy road, it took the bus half an hour to travel eight miles (thirteen kilometers). The air felt extremely dry and thin as we approached the lofty heights of Lalibela.

We were dropped off at the government-run Seven Olives Hotel, but Sarah and I had designs on staying at a private hotel instead. Several boys trailed us a few yards down the road and into the gates of the Asheton Hotel, all the while firing bothersome questions at us. This budget-travelers' destination looked more like a schoolhouse than a hotel. In the rectangular court-yard, poinsettia shrubs, as big as trees, burned red in the highland sun. The boys watched us check in, then followed us to our room and continued to stare as we unpacked.

"Excuse me," I said and shut the door in their faces. Strangers who approached unsolicited in Ethiopia reminded me of telemarketers at home. They were so tedious, so grating, and one became so annoyed by their intrusions, that even before you know what they want—good or bad—you just slam down the phone, or in this case slam the door, before they have the opportunity to get a word in edgewise.

The cement floor of the communal bathroom sloped downward, presumably for drainage. The shower was a nice feature, but the water only came on at 6:00 p.m. and there were no guarantees that even that was a daily occurrence. The sink was as grimy as any found in an auto mechanic's shop and the hot water handle was missing. But through a little opening in the wall, meant as a window, you could see dramatic hillsides towering over the town and catch a few warming rays of sunshine and a cool breeze.

"I'm beyond the backpacking stage," I informed Sarah when I returned to our little cement cell.

"Oh, come on, Julie," she said. "You have to do this occasionally to remind yourself that you're not old."

But I was feeling old, and I was missing the creature comforts of my birthright. My throat felt parched and my skin and lips had become excessively dry.

"It's not like we don't have money," I whined. "Or that we can't get money whenever we need it...."

For all my complaints, there were compensations. A cozy oval dining room had the potential to make up for the bucket baths. The floor was covered with brown and khaki rough fiber rugs. The engraved bar replicated Lalibela's rock-hewn churches. The ceiling was the room's crowning touch, imitating the Debre Birhan Selassie Church in Gondar with rows and rows of little angle faces in pale blue and gold. I noticed, to the amusement of other travelers in the room, that the brass carriage lamps had been installed upside down.

The requisite Ethiopian tourism posters hung on the walls. The most ubiquitous of these boasted "13 Months of Sunshine." Rather than following our Gregorian calendar, Ethiopians follow the Julian calendar, initiated by Julius Caesar in 46 BC. The Julian calendar is comprised of twelve months with thirty days each and an extra month with five or six days, depending on leap year. Their calendar lags seven years and eight months behind the Gregorian calendar, allowing Ethiopia Tourism authorities another fun gimmick; visitors can claim they are nine years younger in Ethiopia than at home.

\* \* \*

There is one reason, and one reason only, to come to a place so frightfully close to heaven and hell as Lalibela: eleven wondrous eight-hundred-year-old churches carved into solid rock, each monolithic and each distinct from the other. Following the decline of Axum as the seat of regional power, a king named Lalibela chose this setting high up in the Lastan Mountains for his capital. With a penchant for religion as well as heights, King Lalibela bankrolled the construction of the rock-hewn churches around Lalibela town. According to legend, this incredible feat was undertaken with the assistance of angels and was intended as a way of concealing the sacred buildings from invaders. Unfortunately, Lalibela's churches, even though ranked as the Eighth Wonder of the World, are generally overlooked by a world that knows their resting place primarily for its past famines, war, and extreme poverty.

Earlier on the bus, Sarah and I had met an elderly British couple, who kindly offered to let us join them in viewing the churches since they were only two and were travelling with their own English-speaking Ethiopian guide. Having neglected to establish a rendezvous point with the Brits, we decided to begin searching for them at Bet Medhane Alem (House of Our Savior), the church nearest our hotel. Upon stepping foot into the compound we were swarmed by hoards of children aspiring to be our guide.

"You have a guide?" one asked standing on a step below us blocking our path.

"Yes, we're meeting up with a group," Sarah replied.

"What group?" he demanded.

"That's none of your business, you little..."

My words trailed off as we descended further into the trench surrounding the church in search of the priest who sells tickets to the sites.

At the bottom of the steps a doe-eyed crazy man assailed us. He followed closely behind as we approached the thirty-six foot (11-meter) high stone building sunk deep into the earth. Bet Medhane Alem, over a hundred feet long and seventy-two wide (thirty by twenty-two meters), is believed to be the largest monolithic rock-hewn structure in the world. Sarah and I attempted to ignore our assailant and to admire the phenomenal church with its twenty-eight carved columns. We circled the church in hopes of soaking in a sense of awe for this human triumph, as well as shaking off our friend. But the man doggedly shadowed us, squawking and gesturing wildly. He was motioning for us to do something.

A crippled boy hobbled over and begged. In a cubby hole carved into a wall, a monk reading a religious book beckoned to us with his own competing squawking sounds, as the lunatic hopped and jumped and signaled in his mimetic way: "Look at the monk! Look at the monk!"

Sarah took a step toward one of the wide-open side doors of the church without removing her shoes, nearly causing the lunatic to explode. When we finally realized there was a shoes-off requirement, the madman wiped his forehead in relief. Philip M. Allen and Aaron Segal, in *The Traveler's Africa* dated 1973, wrote:

> Removing the shoes before entering an Orthodox Church, as in a mosque, is a graceful gesture that few visitors seem to know about. It raises murmurs of approval and smiles....

These days, grubby little boys jockey with each other for the opportunity to become shoe keepers, and crazy men blow a gasket if you don't comply.

We slipped off our shoes at a doorway and gathered them into our arms—no way were we leaving expensive footwear to the mercy of that rabble.

Inside the church the air was cool and calm. We found the British couple and their guide admiring the church's high alter. The shock from the pests and lunatics hovering outside did not wear away easily; I had a hard time concentrating on the interior of the ancient building in which we stood.

Our newly formed group reemerged into the scorching sunlight only to find a pack of beggars sitting on the steps outside the church. To proceed to the second church we had to walk through a tunnel, also filled with beggars. A mass of dingy-brown, from their dust-covered skin and hair to the rags on their backs, the beggars crawled and limped after us shaking outstretched palms and chanting "Santo Christo, Lalibela."

"If I gave just one *birr* to each of these beggars," said the British tourist, "I'd be broke."

We climbed down steps into a mote-like area surrounding the next church. A wafer-thin man with reddened eyes and arms outstretched bobbed in and out of a cubbyhole in the wall, repeating, "I am blind, I am poor, help me. I am blind, I am poor, help me." Indigent women and toddlers blocked our way uttering, "Santo Christo, Lalibela. Santo Christo, Lalibela...." One slender waif with never-combed hair sat as elegantly as a Parisian model in a hole in a sandy wall. She just smiled and stared.

Our tour guide ignored the orgy of penury and began explaining the church's history. A woman followed by two children, lacking any sense of propriety (if there can be any such thing in this mad human cesspool), wandered over to our little group of sanity and chanted in my ear: "Help me, I am poor. Help me, I am poor." She nudged her son in the chest to prompt him to cry. I turned and glared at the boy. He stopped whimpering as suddenly as he had started.

We trudged up and down steps, were secreted through underground tunnels and caves, and were herded in and out of churches. And yet it seemed as though every time we turned a corner, in front of us appeared the same footless boy. I'd seen my share of poverty and deformity in six years living in East Africa, but still found myself totally stunned by this aspect of Ethiopia. What did I expect, I had to ask myself, of a country which only a few years earlier the World Bank claimed was the world's poorest?

By then I was well aware that in Ethiopia the poor migrated to the churches, and the churches tolerated this as a matter of creed. In Lalibela, the same buildings that tourists saw as historical masterpieces and elements of our world heritage, the impoverished saw as places of refuge, and perhaps places of hope. I would never suggest taking away this role from the Ethiopian church, but something needed to be done. It was just that tourists and beggars mix as well as oil and water. One group is out to shake loose and leave behind all the niggling cares of their daily existence; the other cannot escape them.

The omnipresence of the destitute is just one of many problems that need to be addressed by Lalibela tourism authorities. Another is the lack of signs or markers informing tourists where and how to buy tickets, and plaques indicating the names of the churches. This, along with the bewildering maze of passageways and underground tunnels connecting the churches, is what necessitated employing a guide. In Philip Briggs' guidebook to Ethiopia, which I read too late, he advised visitors to pick up a booklet on Lalibela from the Ethiopian Tourism Commission in Addis Ababa.

"You'd be crazy," he accurately warns, "to visit Lalibela without it."

Heaven knows there are already enough crazy people in Lalibela.

Even the more refined guides, like the English-speaking one from a reputable tour company in Addis Ababa accompanying the British couple, possessed scant and spotty information on Lalibela's history. The tourist becomes frustrated at worst, confused at best. And yet, while every young man and child in town was scrambling to hold your shoes or become your guide, you could not find a piece of fresh fruit or a cold drink to save your life. Ethiopian tourism has a long distance to travel.

Winding through one underground passageway we saw a teenage boy curled up in a hole in the wall reading a prayer book aloud in Ge'ez. The ancient language of Ethiopia, Ge'ez was still used for religious purposes, much like Latin has been used by the Roman Catholic Church. The guide told us that the boy was a deacon.

"One less nuisance on the streets," Sarah said and I readily agreed.

Our tour followed a path through an area where monks lived in niches carved into the sides of cliffs with short wooden doors. The doors were locked with heavy chains, which seemed very unmonk-like. Several residents were busy grinding grain using heavy stones. Perhaps it was this hobbit-like housing that gave rise to ancient Greek travelers' imaginative claims that Troglodytes lived in the southern reaches of the known world. While Asmara may have harkened back to the Rome of the 1930s, Lalibela took the traveler back two thousand years.

In *Report on Africa*, Oden Meeker wrote that in the old days in Ethiopia you could spot a holy man "in nearly every cave, on every inaccessible rock ledge and behind every waterfall." This was because the *kahinat*, a collective term for priests, deacons, and some monks, was not a very exclusive club in Ethiopia. In the 1960s, ten to twenty percent of all Amhara and Tigray adult males were priests, and as many as one hundred priests could be attached to the largest of the country's 18,000 or so churches.

Most Ethiopian holy men are peasants with little education beyond what is taught to them during their deaconhood. A boy can only be a deacon into his teenage years, at which point he is deemed "too worldly." Then the young man must decide whether or not to choose the road to priesthood. An Ethiopian Orthodox priest can commit himself to either celibacy or marriage, but divorce or adultery makes the man ritually impure and he looses his ordination. Monks, on the other hand, remain celibate and extremely pious. Some undertake advanced religious studies. Some monks are hermits, while others live in monastic centers, like the one we passed through. Women, as far as I could tell, do not play a large role in the clergy of the Ethiopian Orthodox Church.

Illustrated prayer books, some as old as the twelfth century, were freely displayed on wooden stands beside the church alters. Permitted to leaf through them, the British man was in awe as he turned the parchment pages.

"It's like being able to handle the Gutenberg Bible," said his wife, referring to the first bible ever printed with movable type.

The priests also exhibited the church's ornamented crosses, some made of gold, and ancient prayer sticks. One of these prayer sticks belonged to King Lalibela himself. The priests stood expressionless, as they posed for photographs. They held those incredible treasures as if it were one of the more tiresome requirements of the job.

At one church a beam of sunlight poured through an open side door. Outside the doorframe two elderly men draped in yards of white cloth and carrying wooden staffs sat on a bench. Before them, one of the ancient leather-bound prayer books lay open. Townspeople came to these churches, our guide explained, to pray on the holy days of their favorite saints and angels, imploring them to carry their messages and prayers to God. The old men read and chanted in Ge'ez, occasionally stopping to giggle and tease each other.

One small church, Bet Abba Libanos, was chiseled into the vertical face of a rock. Legend holds that King Lalibela's wife, Meskel Kebra, with the help of angels raised Bet Abba Libanos in one night. The interior was cool and dark. We rested on a wooden bench while the guide directed our attention to a small diamond-shaped light high up on the altar wall.

"It's a magical light," the guide said. "Some kind of radioactive element."

"Bullocks," blurted a tall Scottish hiker who had joined our little group. The Scotsman, standing up, moved his head back and forth slightly to examine the light beam. "It's a hole in the wall," he scowled, "with the sun shining through it."

Confusion broke out in the cavernous building as everyone commenced talking at once. The guide and the priest defended the magical light theory, while the

*Ancient religious texts inside a rock-hewn church in Lalibela*

tourists stood up in turns, moving backward and forward trying to break down the myth empirically.

"This place is such a rip-off," growled the Scotsman's short American companion.

Like all the other nonbelievers, at a certain angle I could clearly make out a wood beam outside the hole in the wall. Somewhat skeptical already, I now had to seriously doubt the guide's earlier information that a large pillar in one of the previously viewed churches emits a mysterious light. The guide told us that ever since it was originally wrapped in cloth centuries ago, no one, not even the priests, was allowed to look at this illuminated pillar. Such blatant fabrications, unfortunately, make questions surrounding the sacred Ark of the Covenant loom even larger.

The Ark of the Covenant is the gold-plated wooden chest in which Moses placed two stone tablets inscribed with the Ten Commandments. According to Ethiopians, the Ark rests in Axum in the sixteenth century Church of Saint Mary of Zion. A monk dedicates his life to protecting the Ark, and he is the only one allowed to see it, although it is always kept wrapped in cloth, for the Ark is believed to be powerful and harmful to those who look upon it.

How did the Ark arrive in Axum? An Ethiopian legend says that one thousand years before the birth of Christ, an Ethiopian queen named Makeda, more commonly known as Queen Sheba, made a pilgrimage to Jerusalem drawn by the renowned wisdom of King Solomon of Israel. The African queen intended to "prove him with hard questions."

"I love him merely on hearing concerning him and without seeing him," Makeda said before setting out on her journey. "And the whole story of him that hath been told to me is to me as the desire of my heart, and like water to a thirsty man."

That Sheba's journey was made is recorded in the bible in *1 Kings 10*: "She came to Jerusalem with a very great retinue," the biblical passage states, "with camels bearing spices, and very much gold, and precious stones....Never again came such an abundance of spices as these which the queen of Sheba gave Solomon." It is the remainder of the Ethiopian version of the story that invites skepticism.

King Solomon, according to Ethiopian accounts, tricked his beautiful visitor into joining him in bed by promising not to force himself upon her if she, in turn, promised not to take any of his property without asking. Then he prepared for her a sumptuous banquet of well-spiced foods. During the night, Queen

Sheba became thirsty and drank from a water vessel at her bedside, at which moment King Solomon accused her of breaking her promise and took her into his bed. The son begat from this union was Menelik I. When Menelik I became a man, he returned to Jerusalem to visit his father. While there, one of his companions stole the Ark of the Covenant from the Holy of the Holies of the Temple in Jerusalem and brought it back to Ethiopia where it remains to this day.

The legend of the Ark, in addition to provoking Ethiopians to its fierce defense, has inspired truck-loads of artwork. Two of the most popular forms are paintings illustrating the story with comic-strip style captioned panels and clay Falasha figurines depicting Solomon and Sheba lying together in bed. If, as some say, God himself chose Ethiopia as the resting-place of the Ark, I can only hope that someday in the future He has another inspired plan for this country.

"Ethiopia is a land," say Ethiopian Airline tickets, "where the great unknown yonder still exists in plenty." Ethiopians love mythology and are hard pressed to separate it from reality. In this smokey, mystical land, it is indeed hard to untangle the two. Take the myth of Gabra Manfas, the patron saint of animals. Gabra Manfas is believed to have lived for 363 years, most of them on top of Mount Zaquella. On this mountain is a cleft rock that even modern-day Ethiopians believe will snap shut when two lovers walk through if their love is untrue. And people of all Ethiopia's religions are said to believe in the evil eye. Called the *buda*, the evil eye's power rests with the lower casts of society. People wear amulets or summon the name of God to protect themselves from this incipient malevolence.

\* \* \*

Sometimes while in Lalibela, I imagined that the incredible historical sights had been flown in by a C-130 military cargo plane and plopped down, lock, stock, and barrel, in the middle of a desperate town as an ingenious method of attracting outsiders with hard cash. Of course, the churches had been there for centuries. The only thing cargo planes had brought in recent years were ton after ton of food aid, and the churches weren't built for outsiders but for the deeply religious locals.

Lalibela lay at the heart of a region infamous for its mid-1980s famine. Initiated by drought in 1984 and 1985, the disaster was exacerbated by a 1986 locust and grasshopper plague, which caused near total crop failure. A civil war in the north made it difficult for agencies to deliver food and supplies. Add a government that was both ineffectual and unwilling to respond appropriately, and you have a catastrophe of biblical proportions. During that period I recall having seen an American comedian on television screaming into a microphone something to the effect: "They don't need grain, they need U-Hauls. They live in a fucking desert! Why don't they get the fuck out of there?" Perhaps Mengistu saw this comedian too, as his government forcibly removed over half a million people from the northern regions to more fertile southern zones.

From 1984 to 1986, an impassioned international relief effort brought 900,000 tons of food to almost eight million people, of whom up to one million died. Ten years later, walking across the same scorched earth, I remembered the baffling, horrific scenes of human suffering and death that flashed across my television screen. Ten years later, with the number of calories available daily to the average Ethiopian even less than it was in 1986, the people still live by such a fragile thread that tragedy of that magnitude does not seem unfathomable at all.

In Lalibela town, residents appeared to be doing their best to betray those demons of the past. Women sat outside their homes grinding grain and braiding each other's hair, while others returned from collecting water. Their houses, clinging to the hillsides, reflected a mix of styles. Some in town sported charming wooden balconies. There were circular mud huts, called *tukuls*, with the peaks of their thatched roofs decorated by broken pots. There were also traditional Tigray houses, *hidmo*, two-story stone structures with stone staircases winding around the outside.

\* \* \*

At sunset, Sarah and I headed for Bet Giorgis (House of Saint George) determined to absorb some of the mystery and enchantment of the land, and to snap a memorable photograph or two. Bet Giorgis was built so deeply into the rocky earth near the edge of a cliff that its roof, shaped into a Greek cross, is level with the ground. The plateau into which the church has been carved grants superb views of the mountains and canyons beyond—a prime site for watching the sun set.

Alas, the children of Lalibela town were out in full force. Sarah made the fatal mistake of talking to them as they followed us down the steps toward the church.

"Get lost," Sarah said. "We do not want you to come with us. You are annoying children."

They were wholly encouraged. "Sojourners in the highlands," wrote Oden Meeker in *Report on Africa*, "complain of increased irritability and hangovers." We had not had an opportunity to test the hangover part yet, but increased irritability we could affirm.

To rid herself of the kids, Sarah's tactic was to sit on a big boulder at the top of the slanted plateau, take a book out of her backpack, and pretend to read. Surely, she figured, this would bore them. Four or five children stood in a line facing Sarah and stared at her reading the book. After about ten minutes, one of the children scooted closer to Sarah and made duck quacking sounds directly into her ear: "Whack, whack-whack, whack, whack-whack."

Miraculously, I had been able to stand under a tree at the lower edge of the plateau all by myself for nearly fifteen minutes. "Whack, whack-whack, whack."

It was reckless, but I couldn't help myself from laughing at Sarah. The children spotted me—uh, oh—a lone *ferenji* standing beside a tree. Like army ants fixed on a tasty morsel, they marched single file down the plateau. Feeling a strange cross of impatience and resignation, I grabbed one of the boys around his waist and counted—one, two, three—as I swung his skinny little body over the edge of the steep cliff. I managed that fake let-go-for-a-second thing without actually letting go. The second time I performed this maneuver—because now it was a great joke, like, "Hey, throw me to a gruesome death! Throw me!"—I swung the boy over the three-story-high hole in the ground into which Bet Giorgis was built. Burning in my brain, as if ancient monks' souls and the rock itself were calling for a live sacrifice, was the strongest desire to actually toss him in. Fortunately, as quickly as these thoughts passed through my head, so did the image of weaving cotton cloth on a primitive loom in a gloomy, over-crowded Ethiopian jail cell.

\* \* \*

Lalibela's children don't just chant "hello" or yell "*ferenji*," both of which are tolerable, even congenial, but they follow you for hours, even after you make it painfully clear that you do not appreciate their company.

"They are so aggressive," Sarah remarked, exasperated.

Like the children, the flies in Lalibela were aggressive and unrelenting. Local guides broke switches off of pepper trees and handed them to us to use as fly-whisks. The pepper switches were effective and gave off a sweet essence, however they had the unpleasant side effect of making your hands sticky. Nothing good came without a price in Ethiopia, or, to employ one of the country's own proverbs: "In Ethiopia where you find honey, you find it on a thorn."

"These people are just mad," the American mountain climber said loudly in the Asheton Hotel dining room that evening. "They're barking mad!" The hikers told us that the best time they'd had in Ethiopia was laughing at day's end at all the ridiculous things that had happened. The two men had just conquered the Simien Mountains, a volcanic range stretching northward from Gondar that UNESCO has designated a world heritage site. Within the Simiens is Ras Deshen, which, at 15,100 feet (4,605 meters), is the fourth highest peak in Africa. In the surrounding 111 square miles (287 square kilometers) of park live three animals found nowhere else in the world—the rare and endangered Simien red fox, the gelada baboon (called, in an article by Linda Waddell in *One World Magazine*, "a cross between a lion and a poodle"), and the Walia ibex, an endangered, thick-horned wild goat. The hikers informed us that the number of visitors to the Simiens increased twentyfold in the last several years, which meant an increase from about ten to a whopping two hundred people annually.

Sarah and I soon discounted the shorter of the two hikers as a pompous ass.

"There is malaria all over Ethiopia. What does altitude have to do with it?" he argued with those of us who said that you couldn't get malaria at high altitudes.

I explained that Nairobi, where I lived for six years, was free of malaria because it was almost a mile high, although there had been rare cases believed caused by lowlanders travelling into Nairobi and carrying malaria with them. He mocked my explanation, his voice getting louder. There is a point when you realize someone is so stubborn and condescending you just give up the conversation and wander off to bed. Had the hiker picked up any guidebook he would have read the simple facts. Says one of mine, "Addis Ababa is above the mosquito zone."

Sarah and I were awakened by what sounded like a bird rolling a rock, over and over again, on the metal roof of the hotel. The usual early morning sounds rushed in: Lalibela's children were awake and yelling, birds sounded exceptionally chatty, roosters were crowing, and the voices of other guests could be heard echoing through the triangular courtyard of the hotel. The mountains were shrouded in a haze as the sun began its daily chore of searing the land.

A Peace Corps volunteer who recently finished her two-year contract in Ghana decided to join Sarah and me for the morning's tour of the remaining churches. Only steps away from our hotel, we jumped directly into the Lalibela fray. Being late for our 9:00 a.m. meeting with the British couple and their guide, we attempted to shortcut through the grounds of the first church we visited the day before. Sarah and I already held tickets good for unlimited visits to all the churches in Lalibela and its environs for as many days as we were there.

At the gate of the Bet Medhane Alem compound the ticket taker materialized. He was a squat, box-shaped man with a worn-out face and old dog eyes, wrapped up like a mummy in a white shawl and a white turban and carrying a wooden staff.

He yelled: "Ticket! Ticket! Ticket!"

The former Peace Corps volunteer pulled out her ticket and handed it to him. He slapped his hand over the face of the ticket.

"What is your name?" he demanded in staccato English.

She replied, "Lori."

"What is your name?" he asked again. Then he shouted, "I.D.! I.D.!" As Lori looked for a piece of identification he continued bellowing, "What is your guide's name?" It was like the scene from the movie *Monty Python and the Holy Grail* where a guard demanded that knights correctly answer several idiotic questions before they were allowed to cross over a bridge:

"What is your name?"

"What is your favorite color?"

"What is the airspeed of an African swallow?"

"Oh forget it," said Sarah.

"Let's just walk the long way around," I suggested. It was too early in the morning for this type of hullabaloo. Sarah and I proceeded through town. After rounding a corner, we looked back and saw an unlikely mob trailing behind us: the two hikers in floppy straw hats towering above an entourage of local boys prattling out of turn at the foreigners, the heavy-set ex-Peace Corps volunteer dawdling at the back of the mass, and the ticket man in a frenzy, weaving in and out of the group, hopping and shouting and gesturing.

The two of us found the back entrance to the church and waved up at the Brits who were waiting. Just then the ticket man broke away from the moveable rabble and hurled himself like a discus at Sarah and me.

"Ticket! Ticket!" he roared, risking spontaneous combustion. We showed him our tickets. He gestured like, "Oh, okay. Have a nice visit."

Without question, my favorite moment in Lalibela came when we were all alone—that is, alone in a group of seven tourists and one tour guide—holding hands in a chain, making our way through the pitch blackness of an underground tunnel. We passed instructions down the line:

"Walk straight."

"We are going down an incline now."

"Watch for the big rock on the left."

"Lower your head."

It reminded Sarah of Scooby Doo. I thought of the Space Mountain roller coaster at Disneyland—for the few precious moments of the dark ride I was able to totally forget where I was, and, in the case of Lalibela, how little I wanted to be there.

The Brits' guide asked me if I was enjoying Ethiopia. Bad question to ask at that particular moment in time.

*A lone beggar child inside the rocky passageways connecting underground churches in Lalibela*

"No," I replied point blank. "I wouldn't suggest for anyone to come here, not for several years anyway."

As any loyal Ethiopian would, he argued feverishly in his country's favor. I fought just as hard to defend the independent tourist's point of view.

"The country is beautiful," I agreed, "but the gorgeous sights don't outweigh the hassles."

Keeping in mind that Ethiopia's natural scenery and historical sights are truly extraordinary, we are talking *big* hassle factor here.

"But many people enjoy," he retorted. "They like to talk to the people."

"Yes," I agreed. "They like to meet locals, but they don't want children staring into their faces when they try to watch the sun set over the hills."

I thought about how the sun shines on Africa, strong and fierce like a warrior, raising blessings in abundance from the earth. Enough for all, but not shared by all. I mentioned that Eritreans didn't appear as poor as Ethiopians.

"Their economy is no good," said the guide.

"True, the people may have less," I replied. "But they don't act poor. They seem more satisfied."

"Beggars are collected," he said, "and taken away or put in jail. It's not allowed, begging." The guide did admit to huge gaps between the rich and the poor in Ethiopia. "There are fifty million people," he explained, "It's hard to control them all."

In fact, there are closer to sixty million people in Ethiopia (eighteen times that of Eritrea) spread throughout plateaus, woodlands, valleys, and deserts in one of the world's bigger nations (twenty-first largest by area), with poor communications and few roads—they would be difficult to control.

"Discipline," I continued. "This is the word used so often to describe Eritreans, and it is exactly what is lacking here."

The guide started to break down, "I try to tell the children this."

I pushed on, "But it is the parents who are to blame. They must care enough to discipline their own children."

"They are trying to change this. Anyway," he finally conceded, "I see your point. It's true."

Walking back to our hotel after a long, sticky day of church viewing, Sarah and I passed a man on the roadside who sat on his butt bone, holding his legs up in the air, at the end of which were mere stumps. He jiggled his hand at us in search of *birr*. According to the government rehabilitation agency, this man was just one of an estimated five million disabled Ethiopians, many disabilities having occurred as a result of the Eritro-Ethiopian war. I actually had to force myself to break away from our conversation and look twice at him to let the horror of his deformity sink in. In front of the walls of the hotel a crazy woman in a dirty, kelly green dress—that looked suspiciously similar to a school uniform—was singing loudly and pounding her bare feet into the dusty road. She shook her shoulders violently, the way Ethiopian dancers do. It didn't faze me. It frightened me how quickly I was becoming desensitized to the crippled, the deformed, and the mad that populate Ethiopia. Nonetheless, the next day, unable to face Lalibela another time, Sarah and I refused to leave our hotel room until the bus for the airport arrived in the afternoon.

\*   \*   \*

Parched throats, flaking skin, and dust in our hair, we sat in the stuffy chicken shed waiting for that Twin Otter chariot with its princely pilot to come and whisk us away. This was way too much like the relief and development work I used to do: the stark landscape reminiscent of northern Kenya, the cramped, noisy planes carrying passengers to remote sites like southern Sudan, the uncomfortable accommodation and bucket baths too much like Zaire. Rethinking my concept of vacation, I wondered why I didn't restrict my holidays to the beaches of Florida, the Bahamas, or Thailand, like saner people. Shorter trips, more luxuries. In the heat of Lalibela airport, I pronounced myself guilty of romanticizing Africa. Maya Angelou did it. African-Americans do it all the time. Many of my friends do it. I am in good company anyway. I muttered words I thought I'd never hear myself say:

"I can't wait to get back to Addis."

# Awash

*One is born. One dies. The land increases....*

— Oromo proverb

After our return to Addis Ababa from Lalibela, Jonas, our companion and defender from Bahar Dar and Gondar, invited Sarah and me to attend a family gathering at his niece's house. He and a brother, also visiting from Washington, D.C., picked us up at our hotel in a Volvo with leather interior that they had imported to use whenever they are in town. Similarly flashy cars filled the driveway inside his niece's high-walled compound.

The living room buzzed with warm conversation. Jonas's well-dressed relatives grinned with polished smiles and showed sincere interest in his new friends, making us feel rather at home. The dining table was laid out with an elaborate buffet that included potato salads, meat salads, fried vegetables, fried meats, Ethiopian spicy stews, and *injera*. A chef, in a white uniform and Pillsbury dough boy hat, presided over the affair, hands folded behind his back.

It was one good-looking, high-powered family. Surely the men held good jobs too, but it was the women—African women—who most interested me: one was an Ethiopian Airlines hostess, another imported used cars from Germany, and a third represented Bayer Aspirin in Ethiopia.

Sarah and I had popped open our eyes that very same morning in a bleak hotel room in a wretched village built into the shoulder of a mountain about as far away as anyone could imagine from twentieth century civilization. Now, our evening was being played out virtually at the peak of the country's social elegance. Ethiopia, once again, was most charitable at night.

After the meal, the party moved outside to the front lawn where a bonfire blazed. Having suffered all day with a scratchy throat, I began having labored breathing, which rapidly escalated to frightening proportions. Through gasps for air, I was forced to ask Jonas if he would take us back to the hotel where an inhaler was in my luggage.

The following morning we awoke to discover the curse of Lalibela upon us. Sarah and I reviewed our combined ailments. I had bronchitis (hence the breathing problem), and the palms of my hands were covered with stinging red dots: I suspected heat rash. Sarah had a fever and giardia (you've heard of Delhi belly, now meet Lalibelly), a nauseating malady manifesting itself with sulfurous burps, intestinal gas, and frothy diarrhea. We both had little itchy bites all over our bodies thought to be from bedbugs. The Holiday Hotel staff had been so sweet and helpful—one porter refused a tip after lugging four suitcases up several flights of stairs and then returning with bottles of Gouder and Ambo—that neither Sarah nor I could summon the nerve to alert them to a possible infestation. Instead, we had slept on top of the covers.

Two of Jonas's family members telephoned to inquire about my health and to help me locate a good

doctor. Sarah and I set out on our search for the rec-
ommended Buruk Clinic. We hopped in a minibus,
locally known as a *wiyiyit.* Unlike Kenyan public
transport in which there is always room for three or
four more, Ethiopians take overcrowding to heart.
Because the mini-bus carried one extra passenger, the
tout rode through downtown with his head tucked
between his knees.

Our next mode of transport was a taxi. The taxi
turned a sharp corner and Sarah's door flew open. She
let out a gasp and pulled it shut again. When the taxi
stopped, we realized that none of the passenger doors
opened from the inside. The elderly cab driver got out
and walked around the taxi to free us. When he did
this, the car started rolling downhill. Sarah tugged on
the emergency brake. It flung upward like a limp
noodle. The old taxi man hustled back into the driver's
seat and jammed the car into gear.

"Nothing at all works properly!" Sarah announced
through laughter.

We finally saw a sign that said Brook Clinic, not
Buruk Clinic and immediately realized we had mis-
understood the Ethiopian accent. The Brook Clinic
presented a fine example of an Ethiopian oddity—
methodical chaos. Twenty or so patients were seated
outdoors on benches near the x-ray room quietly
waiting for the lunch break to end. When the door
swung open after lunch hour, the patients rushed
forward and pushed inside. I thought the whole system
had fallen into total disarray. But within minutes
everyone returned to their same seats and resumed
patiently and silently waiting.

Although ill health cannot be dictated, one should
try to avoid becoming sick in Ethiopia. In Addis Ababa,
even though doctors are generally well trained, there
are but a few hundred of them. And the *Ethiopian
Herald* reported only eight ambulances for the city's
four to six million residents, giving a whole new
meaning to the practice of triage. As of 1990, in the
country as a whole, there was only one doctor for every
32,650 people. An estimated seventy percent of the

population had to walk three days to the nearest health center. Only ten percent of baby deliveries in 1993, according to World Health Organization figures, were attended by trained personnel. If I were to die at the age of the average Ethiopian, at thirty-five I was only twelve years away from my demise.

To be treated by one of the capital city's best doctors, Dr. Mekonnen, cost me 25 *birr* (less than US $4). Apparently, that price was high enough to exclude most residents, because I didn't wait long to see the doctor, and, as best as I could tell, I was not given preferential treatment as a foreigner.

*  *  *

Departing from the Holiday Hotel at 6:30 a.m. on a Sunday morning completely disoriented the staff. Tesfaye and Kidane happened to be driving south to the border town of Moyale on the same day that Sarah and I were heading east into Moslem Ethiopia, to the French-designed city of Dire Dawa and the walled city of Harar. They offered us a lift part way along our 308-mile (571-kilometer) journey, but they were leaving at sunrise. Groggy and disheveled, the receptionist stirred from his slumber on a couch in the lobby. The barman was awakened somewhere in a back room to come pop open two cold bottles of soda: apparently, it was much too early to expect coffee.

As the car descended the one-and-a-half-mile-high plateau on which Addis Ababa sits, both Tesfaye and I complained that our ears hurt. Eventually, Sarah and I would travel down to about 3,000 feet (914 meters) nearing the border with Somalia.

On the southeastern outskirts of Addis Ababa, the scenery suddenly mutated from industrial zone to bucolic splendor. Spread along both sides of the highway were golden valleys dotted with stubby trees similar to those in Doctor Seuss's *Horton Hatches the Egg*. *Teff*, the grain from which *injera* is made, marches across the land in neat mounds that look like downy knolls beckoning field hands to dive in. Horse-drawn carts clop down the road. Kidane called the land "Ethiopia's breadbasket," and in better times Ethiopia itself was known as the "Breadbasket of the Middle East."

In keeping with their boundless generosity, Tesfaye and Kidane treated Sarah and me to omelets and coffee at the Hora Ras Hotel in Debre Zeit, about an hour's drive outside of Addis Ababa. We ate on a large veranda overhanging Lake Hora. Lake Hora was a glossy pool at the bottom of a crater in the Great Rift Valley, a trench in the Earth stretching from Mozambique through East Africa all the way to the Middle East's Jordan Valley.

"This was one of Haile Selassie's palaces," explained Tesfaye. "He had to have a palace everywhere he went."

At the end of Selassie's rule, there were fifteen royal palaces in Ethiopia. These days monkeys rule the old palace at Debre Zeit, one of which was sitting on a wall beside us hiccuping. The hiccuping monkey with florescent blue testicles began a confrontation with Tesfaye that could not be resolved by throwing scraps of food—the monkey just wanted to fight. Another larger monkey sat further along the wall munching on bread, completely unperturbed.

Tesfaye managed to ward off the monkey and launched into one of his many theories, this time tackling sexism in Muslim societies. "Their women don't lead a normal life," he said. Tesfaye always spoke tongue-in-cheek with a proverbial twinkle in his eye. "They stay inside all the time. They demand lots of special foods and gold from their husbands so that the man can't afford to take any more wives."

An Oromo proverb states, "With one wife the heart is warmed, with the other the kettle is warmed."

Why, I asked, are there are so many Eritreans doing business in Addis Ababa? Tesfaye explained that it stemmed from the days of the Empire when Amharas were mainly interested in acquiring land and ruling over the masses. Recall the proverb: "The Amhara is to rule, not to be ruled." Meanwhile, someone had to take care of trade and commerce, so Eritreans and Ethiopian Muslims primarily filled that role. In addition, imperial subjects needed means to pay heavy taxes extracted by royal families. Eritrean Muslims, Tesfaye said, are especially good business people, having acquired sharp business acumen from years of interaction with Turks, Arabs, and, more recently, Italians.

As we drove, the signboards along the roadside changed quite noticeably. Instead of employing bewildering Amharic or Arabic characters these signs used Latin script, but the words were just as indecipherable. We had entered Oromia land. Locals flashed brownish, decaying teeth at us in broad, genuine smiles, which made me suspect there weren't a lot of Oromia dentists.

This region has long been a center of discontent for the twenty-two million plus Oromo people. Constituting forty percent of the country's population, the Oromo are the largest of Ethiopia's more than one hundred ethnic groups. In the past referred to as Gallas (this term is considered disparaging and is no longer used), the Oromo have spread themselves throughout Ethiopia's middle section, from the western border with the Sudan across Addis Ababa east to Harar and south into northern Kenya. In Kenya they are known by different names, such as Gabbra, Borana, and Orma. Traditionally the Oromo were a pastoral people, a lifestyle most southern Oromo still adhere to, while the northern Oromo have become farmers. They speak a Cushitic language also called Oromo, or more properly Oromiffa, and, judging by the signboards, believe in liberal use of vowels. One of our group suggested a linguistic deal: swap Oromiffa vowels for Croat consonants.

Despite being the second largest ethnic group in Africa (after the Hausa of West Africa), the Oromo remain little known outside the Greater Horn of Africa region. Their obscurity might partly be explained by this excerpt from Asafa Jalata's recent paper, "The

Struggle for Knowledge: The Case of Emergent Oromo Studies," in *African Studies Review*, September 1996:

> The Ethiopian knowledge elite have treated the Oromo as historical objects or have ignored them because of their subordination and powerlessness....some Ethiopianists argued that the Oromo are a people without history and civilization.

Fortunately, at the end of the twentieth century the human race is enlightened enough to know that there are no people on earth without history or civilization, and we recognize such statements as machinations of the human mind that allow one group to justify domination or oppression of another.

"This government is very smart," remarked Tesfaye. "They went to the Oromos and said, 'What is it you want?' The Oromos replied that they wanted to use their own language, using Latin script. Under Mengistu they weren't allowed to use Oromo. This government said, 'Okay, go ahead. Just don't shoot anybody.' Before they were adamant about their language. Now they're not as concerned. People are like children. You tell them they can't have something, and they will pester you for it. Once allowed to have it, they lose interest."

Tesfaye and Kidane dropped us off at the Nazareth taxi park and continued their 400 mile (740 kilometer) journey to Moyale on the Kenyan border, while Sarah and I boarded public transport toward Sodore.

On both minibuses it took to get to Sodore the passengers insisted that the windows be sealed as tight as Tupperware. The temperature was at least eighty degrees Fahrenheit (twenty-six degrees Celsius) and was flat out hot. Sarah and I were sweating rivulets and feeling claustrophobic. We tried to open the window in front of us a teensy crack, but a young man reached over and slammed it shut.

"The draft will disturb her," he said and put his arm around his girlfriend who wore a thick wool sweater and a headscarf.

Was she insane? It was a sauna in there! Sarah
and I could see sweat dripping down other people's
faces and necks. But no, they would rather sweat like
a pork roast in a Dutch oven than risk catching their
death of cold from a little fresh air. No one considered
the fact that maybe twenty-one people crammed
raisin-like into a van, all breathing the same stuffy air
and circulating germs might be a more probable cause
of illness.

Sodore Spa is a popular weekend getaway for Addis
Ababa residents and this Sunday was no exception. It
was rather off-putting. A mob in a pool is never too
appealing, even if the pool is Olympic-sized and fed by
hot springs. As in Massawa, I noticed women wearing
underwear under their swimsuits. The holidaymakers
had brought along boomboxes and blithely disregarded
the fact that their speakers were blown and their cassette tapes trashed.

Tucked away in the woods, behind the hotel, we
discovered a public bathing area. Scalding water
blasted out of large metal pipes into two sunken
shower areas, divided by the sexes. On our side, we
found women standing ankle-deep in the burning
water. They were topless, but wore underpants, and
were vigorously spreading suds over their curvy brown
bodies. Aha! Now we understood why the traders who
descended upon the buses en route to Sodore were
selling soap. One Ethiopian beauty sat on the concrete
ledge soaping her perfectly constructed body, watching us struggle with the water; her impassive face was
like that of a porcelain doll. The water was so blister-
ing that Sarah and I could barely manage to plunge a
big toe in, let alone position our whole bodies under
the powerful streams gushing out of the wall. Some of
these springs are hot enough, reportedly, that locals
boil maize in them.

By late afternoon the crowds started to disperse,
and Sodore became the little scrap of paradise that we
had been searching for in this tumultuous land. Sarah
and I went for a walk along the Awash River.
Somewhere along that same river valley, archaeolo-

gists found the fossil remains of the earliest upright walking hominids, our oldest human ancestors. Along that very river, four million years earlier, human kind as we know it began. Back then our ancestors busied themselves forging sharp tools out of sticks and stones so that they could crack open nuts and dig tubers from the ground. These days we busy ourselves assembling spaceships and computer chips.

The river was murky brown, but it was bounteous and flowed bracingly toward the east over rocky outcrops. Water seeped up through the earth along the footpaths.

"Water everywhere!" said Sarah. "Like it should be!"

We were still recovering from the dryness and insanity of Lalibela. Immense palm fronds draped over the river. Cactus, fir trees, fruit groves, and the woody vines of bougainvillaea garnished the land. Monkeys crisscrossed our path, scampering up and down trees, while tiny black insects nipped at our skin. The peaks of flame-colored termite mounds poked above the bushes. We caught a fleeting glimpse of a mongoose-shaped creature scurrying into the underbrush.

Over 850 species of birds have been recorded in Ethiopia—nearly one-tenth of all bird species in the world, and many of them were swooping, cooing and hooting around us. There were bee eaters with bright green and yellow bodies, blue heads, and ebony slashes across their eyes like Zorro. There were iridescent blue and violet starlings, and mousebirds with crested heads and long tails that looked like advertisement banners trailing behind single-prop airplanes that buzz Florida beaches. There were masses of pigeons belting out haunting cries.

The larger birds were represented by ibis wading in the river, with their long slim pointed beaks, Egyptian geese with mahogany, black, and white feathers, and something resembling an eagle. Any small black bird I saw I insisted was a tit. The white-backed black tit is one of Ethiopia's 29 endemic birds, and I wanted to be able to claim I'd seen one.

"Julie, those are *swallows*," Sarah said each time, repeatedly dashing my hopes.

We spotted several hoopoes—the quintessential African bird with its Zebra-striped hind end and brown breast that looks like Ugandan barkcloth. We tormented a plover, with its handsome black, white, and brown torpedo-shaped body, by moving near and away and near again. The plover waddled across the ground on its stilt legs, its crazed cry reaching fever pitch and sounding like a metal worker beating tin. The cry faded as we moved away again. An unseen bird—perhaps a turaco—let out a raucous ca-ca, ca-ca, capping the experience as a true jungle walk. It felt as if we were, in fact, frolicking in the gardens of the first humans. Standing there, overjoyed by the lovely natural setting, forced me to ponder the sappy sentiment that nuts and tubers might be all humans need, really, to be happy.

Our eyes were drawn upward where we heard a commotion in a tree. A group of monkeys was terrorizing a flock of birds.

"I've never seen that before," I commented, "monkeys fighting with birds."

Sarah looked unfazed.

"*Ethiopian* monkeys and birds," she reminded me, and we realized it was the first fight we had witnessed all day.

We sat beside the river on large smooth rocks and dangled our feet into the cool water. Only half-jokingly, I threw stones into the depths near Sarah's feet to check for crocodiles. The stones reemerged on the surface.

"They're floating!" Sarah was shouting above the river's noise. "It's pumice stone!"

Joyfully, we sat beside the river giving ourselves pedicures as the sun began to slip away.

\* \* \*

With the coming of night, the swimming pool was abandoned, except for a few couples amorously entangled in shadowy corners. The water temperature was perfect. I floated on my back, my skin blue from the reflection of flourescent lamps attached to the trees. On the lawn, a group of young adults each posed in turn looking through the crook of a tree as one of their party used movie lights and a video camera to film them. They were completely oblivious to the *ferenji* floating in the middle of the pool examining the constellations brilliantly laid out in the sky. I felt a sense of relief when I measured that an entire day had passed without any children running after us yelling, "Hey mister! Yellow, Yellow!" No throngs of youth calling out, "Where are you from? What is your job?"

\* \* \*

Sarah and I were awakened early by monkeys marauding in the trees and romping along the hotel balconies. At 7:00 a.m. on Monday morning the Sodore Spa pool and lawn were deserted and I was able to swim solo through the steam rising up from the water. We made an early start for the bus. Where the bus stops, just outside the concrete archway welcoming visitors to Sodore Spa, we counted thirteen other passengers and felt certain we would get a seat. A group of boys played soccer in a dirt patch off to the side. When the bus pulled up, at least thirty people rushed out of some alternative world and all the soccer players were would-be passengers too. Luckily, it was a big bus, holding five people across each row, so we were able to push our way on.

Sarah and I became bored with cramped buses by the time ours arrived at Awash town and decided to alight there for the night. We checked into a double room at Saint George's Hotel. (I now think of that name as a cruel pun; prisons in East Africa used to be known as King George's Hotel.) The hotel faced the main road, which happens to be the only tarmac road in Awash and is probably the only paved surface for hundreds of miles around. According to *CIA Factbook* estimates, in 1995 Ethiopia had 17,611 miles (28,360 kilometers) of road, but only fifteen percent of those were paved.

Our room cost the equivalent of $US 3, and as they say back home, you get what you pay for. The shower ran cold, nonetheless it was invigorating in the heat. After downing a thick, refreshing mix of papaya and avocado juice served with a lime wedge we ventured out into Awash town.

A diminutive man wearing sandals made from old tires, a plaid Somali-style waist wrap, a blazer, and a turban, greeted us on the hotel stairs. One hand held a wooden staff while the other was free to shake our hands vigorously. He took a little plastic package from his breast pocket and transferred it to the breast pocket of my T-shirt. It contained chunks of worthless quartz that he seemed to be trying to pass off as precious stones. I attempted to give the package back to the man, but he would have none of it and followed Sarah and me into the street.

We wandered first into the local market, a slap-dash collection of stick and thatch stalls erected alongside the main road. Our newest Ethiopian companion attempted to direct where we walked and which way we looked, grunting and gesturing for us to follow him this way or that. Sarah and I had already kicked into shopping mode, however, so we were not about to be herded around like that man's goats.

At one large stall in a corner of the market we purchased brightly colored woven baskets and small clay pots. A *haboob*, dust devil, kicked up out of nowhere and spun down the narrow pathways of the market. Voices raised in alarm as women shielded their heads with their arms and shawls. A teenage girl, whom I had not even noticed standing beside me, threw her black shawl over both of our heads, transforming it into a tent. With the dust storm over, our male companion quite forcefully took our purchases from us and stuffed them into plastic bags. We were suspicious of this character's motives on the one hand, but on the other hand he did prove to be useful as a human fly swatter—he kept pesky kids at bay by throwing rocks at them. He was, however, a bit too fervent with this task and angered several of the market women. Sarah and I hustled out of the market.

Next stop was the CARE office. We were looking for someone who spoke English well enough to give us advice on how best to catch the next bus to Dire Dawa. We had been told earlier, though several hours too late, that the easiest method was to catch buses at Nazareth, many kilometers back, where they began their eastward journey. More or less, they said, "You can't get there from here." By the time buses stopped at Awash it was a matter of luck as to whether there would be any empty seats. Berhane, a local administrator at the CARE office, proved helpful and easily accepted an invitation to join us for dinner. We were pretty confident that someone from this remote field office would enjoy accompanying us that evening, as there was not much by way of diversion in Awash town.

The human fly swatter remained close beside us throughout the visit to CARE. No one at CARE could successfully communicate to him that we wanted to walk alone. I don't think anyone spoke his language. In desperation, we ducked into a Christian church compound figuring that he was a Muslim, and that this maneuver might scare him away. Using rudimentary Italian, I explained to an elderly man standing beside the church that we wanted to rest awhile inside the courtyard in attempt to ditch our now very unwanted follower. Some arguing broke out between the two men. The guy was unshakable.

Resigned to being escorted, we carried on through the town's dusty backstreets. After dodging a drunken man who stormed out of a bar and barreled toward us like a heat-seeking missile a little off course, we entered a different marketplace, this one bordered by permanent buildings. Men, who looked Somali to me, sat under canopies chewing *chaat* as cows chew their cud. Known as *miraa* in Kenya, this green stem produces a mildly stimulating effect and suppresses one's appetite.

A madwoman with wild eyes, parched lips, and green foam seeping out of the corners of her mouth (from *chaat*) ran toward us, screaming. We were getting used to this sort of behavior. Upon recognizing our companion, the woman immediately quieted down. She rested a skeletal arm on his shoulder, and the two chatted affectionately in their unidentified language. We already suspected that our guide might have been a bit mad, but now we could safely conclude that not only was he crazy, he was the Pied Piper of the Loony Tunes.

Upon returning to Saint George's Hotel, we indicated to the madman, still in tow, that our journey together was over. We would be going to our room by ourselves. That seemed to us the most reasonable of requests. No, he shook his head vehemently. No, no, no. He was determined to accompany us to some unknown bitter end.

"No, no, no," Sarah and I responded and shook our heads just as ardently, demanding that he give us our shopping bags.

"Coming with us to our room is completely out of the question," we said in a language that he did not know, but by inference should have understood.

A sophisticated-looking man sat on the veranda quietly sipping coffee. We somehow discovered that he spoke English and whatever local language it was that the certifiable character spoke, so we forced the patron out of his relaxed contemplation.

"Tell him it was nice to spend time with him," I pleaded. "But now we must be alone."

"And tell him to give us our bags," Sarah added.

The hotel proprietress soon joined in the fracas, as did several people off the street.

"What does he want?" We were anxious for the coffee drinker to explain to us what was happening. "Is he mad?"

"He's not mad," the man replied. "It's his culture."

We threw out for translation several reasons for not wanting him in our room:

"We are tired and want to be alone."

"We are women, and it is not proper for a man to join us in our room."

"We didn't ask him to come with us."

But, frankly, our opinions did not matter. As we had experienced elsewhere in Ethiopia, the issue was no longer about our desires, or us, it had become a local matter.

Besieged on all sides, the madman accidentally dropped our plastic bags to the ground, potentially breaking our pots. Now he had done it! It was one matter to violate our personal space, but no man would come between Sarah and me and our shopping.

"Hang on there!" we yelled, glaring at him, and with one quick thrust toward him, we grabbed our bags.

At this juncture, the hotel proprietress yanked us both through the hotel doors and locked them behind us. Safely in the hotel courtyard we waited for at least twenty minutes for the situation to settle. Sarah ventured back to the cafe to get some bottled water, only to find the brouhaha still in full swing. The proprietress instructed Sarah to give her two *birr*, which the lunatic snatched off the bar, and then Sarah was shoved back down the stairs to our place of exile.

For the second time in Ethiopia we had become prisoners of a dilapidated hotel room, the only thing separating us from the madness of the masses who dwell outside. A few minutes later a young man knocked on the door.

"Don't be scared," he said. "It is okay now."

He told us that the police had been called to bundle away our first Awash friend.

\* \* \*

Once again, nighttime mellowed even the hottest, dustiest, and most bizarre of Ethiopian towns. Lovely breezes stirred up the tepid evening air. People strolled casually along the town's wide tarmac road, stepping aside gingerly when cargo trucks barreled along toward the port of Djibouti. Lit by dim neon lights, low voices murmuring and laughing, the town was reminiscent of the ambiance at family campgrounds in America.

It happened to be Muslim Id-al-Fitr, the night when the moon is sighted ending the month of fasting known as Ramadan. In the evening around 6:00 p.m. men poured out of the main mosque and headed home to participate in the annual celebrations. Shops remained open late, allowing townspeople to browse for new clothes to don during the four or more days of festivities. Firecrackers popped off throughout the town, and singing voices rose above the drone of the muezzin who was reading a sermon over the Mosque's loud speakers.

Berhane from the CARE office brought his friend Dawit, the young principal of a nearby school, to join us for dinner and drinks. The restaurant that they favored was at another hotel, where wooden chairs and low tables sat in a dirt courtyard. We ordered one platter with tibs—chunks of spiced beef and sautéed onion—and another loaded with vegetables for Sarah. Dinner conversation touched on Ethiopian politics, with Berhane and Dawit listing the positive and negative aspects of their new government. They quickly acknowledged the country's current state of peace as the most positive factor, but dissented along the lines of power sharing. The Tigray ethnic group makes up a substantial portion of Ethiopia's national government, which many perceived as favoring that region of the country. Berhane and Dawit cited the construction of international airports in Tigray locations, for example Gondar and Lalibela, as cases in point. This charge of official favoritism is not to be taken lightly. Because the new government has not effectively embraced Ethiopia's other ethnic groups—several of whom boycotted the 1995 elections—many of them are engaged in some form of liberation struggle. In Africa, it is called tribalism, in Europe ethnic clashes, but those terms only mask reality—in Ethiopia as elsewhere racism continues to rear its ugly head.

I asked the obvious: "Are you two Amharic?"

Berhane and Dawit threw their heads back in uncomfortable laughter and replied, "Yes, yes!"

According to our dinner companions, many elderly people in Ethiopia yearned for the old days of the empire under Haile Selassie.

"Life was better then," one of them reasoned. "Everything was cheaper."

"That was thirty years ago!" Sarah and I said virtually in unison. "The whole world was cheaper."

Berhane shook his head, and continued, "But people are uneducated here. They don't know this."

Clinging to romantic notions of the old empire seemed ludicrous. Travel writer Charlie Pye-Smith in *The Other Nile* described Ethiopia in 1975, just one year after the fall of the emperor, as a decaying, disease-ridden country. I doubt that state of misery developed overnight. Under Selassie's reign, only three percent of the total population attained a high school education and only ten percent could read and write.

In the two decades of the Mengistu regime, the number of high school graduates rose to just fifteen percent—not exactly a glowing commendation for Marxism in Africa either. The Mengistu regime can, however, point to the small but significant success of raising the literacy rate from ten to 32.7 percent by 1990.

According to a World Bank 1996 press release, the current government led by Meles Zenawi cut defense spending from thirty-one to seven percent of the national budget and doubled spending on education. Still, in 1995, UNESCO reported a 35.5 percent adult literacy rate and a USAID report to Congress in 1996 claimed that only twenty percent of Ethiopian children were enrolled in primary school.

Ironically, partly because Ethiopia has one of the lowest education levels in Africa and because only about one percent of the population reads newspapers and magazines regularly, people can continue to dream of former days of imperial greatness unencumbered by the discrepancies of erudition. At any rate, often in these matters one deals not so much with facts as with emotions.

Another complaint leveled against the current regime was that press freedoms were not protected. The Committee to Protect Journalists agrees: in March 1996 the committee reported that Ethiopia held thirty-one journalists in prison, the second highest rate in the world after Turkey.

Berhane told us that he had been selected by the American Embassy for a diversity visa. A Sudanese friend living in Atlanta planned to sponsor him and his wife. I always express reservations when middle-class Africans talk of emigrating to America. In Africa, if you make it to the middle class you are miles above the heap, unlike in America where middle class implies the bulk of the population. In Africa, being middle class confers membership into a pretty select club, deemed middle class only because there is an upper echelon of people who are much richer; I mean rich rich. A middle class African generally has a decent job, lives in a fairly spacious house, maybe drives a car, has a live-in housekeeper who doubles as nanny, sends his or her kids to fairly good schools, perhaps owns a plot of land in the home village, and can afford to take the whole family out for a meal and drinks each Sunday. Family and friends, compatriots and ethnic brothers and sisters are around all the time, providing a far-reaching social support system. Transport this same person to America, and, in most cases, he or she becomes just another struggling, anonymous, working class slob, lost somewhere in the bottom rungs of America's huge middle class.

Berhane admitted to having heard only good things about America and initially welcomed an insider's opinion of the negative aspects.

"People think you can pluck money from trees," I began.

"Something like that," he agreed.

My list of negatives was grueling: high cost of living, long working hours and few holidays, competitive society, high crime rates, and—compared with Africa—

people are not as sociable. Also, only the wealthiest can afford full-time housekeepers or nannies.

Berhane interjected to cancel my last point. "Ethiopians send for an old mother when they have children," he said.

It was time to be blunt. Racism. "The majority of Americans will not care if you are Ethiopian, much less Amharic," I said. "They will see you as black."

The distressed look on his face showed that he was beginning to get the picture.

"And salaries?" he asked.

I calculated a monthly salary based on minimum wage and started to subtract rent, food, etc.

"No, never mind that," he interrupted again. He wanted to return to the positive aspects.

Cheap cars and good living conditions were the first things that came to my mind. He seemed genuinely pleased when I explained that if the water didn't run hot and cold twenty-four hours a day a tenant had major cause for complaint. Such a luxury would be unheard of in Ethiopia.

I could see that the American Dream remained alive and well in Berhane. What were long working hours and a little discrimination from a few prejudiced Americans, as compared with the abject poverty, limited opportunity, and uncertain future in his land? I was sure that Berhane figured he would be discriminated against anyway in Ethiopia, as long as another ethnic group remained at the helm. And I remembered the excitable way a Ghanaian friend back home recounted his first impressions of America.

"I saw a high school parking lot, and it was full of cars," he said, "Cars! High school kids had cars!" One can never downplay the lure of economic security.

Upon my advice, Sarah sprayed the bed sheets with repellent since the hotel didn't provide mosquito nets and the barred window had no screen. The spray had an odor so noxious that I had to squeeze my face through the window bars to inhale fresh air. Double oil tankers whizzed through the sleepless town on their way to the seaports. Aster Aweke's beautiful, shrill voice drifted down from the speakers of the hotel's rooftop bar. The muezzin's chanting blared from the mosque's sound system and the faithful answered en masse throughout the night.

# Harar and
# Dire Dawa

*Anticipate the good so that you may enjoy it.*

— Ethiopian proverb

At six o'clock in the morning Awash town had finally fallen quiet. Like vagabonds loitering into the dawn, pink and blue neon lights glowed from low buildings that stretched alongside the Addis Ababa to Djibouti highway. The outline of a craggy mountain range in the distance was a stunning backdrop to the town's mosque with its smooth, wide, sea green dome and skyward reaching minaret. Trucks continued to rumble down the road piled high with sacks of grain. One truck had two used cars strapped on top of the sacks.

It was 203 miles (376 kilometers) from Awash to Dire Dawa. This translated into seven and a-half hours in another hot, crowded Ethiopian bus speeding across stark landscape along gravel roads. So much dust seeped into the cabin of the bus that passengers wrapped scarves and clothing around their noses and mouths, like impromptu surgical masks. During some segments of the journey it seemed as though my spinal cord might jar loose. At other times it felt like we are locked inside a Finnish sauna. The passengers' heads bobbed up and down as they faded in and out of bouts of steamy sleep.

The farther away we traveled from Awash, the more rough looking the people, the more crowded the bus, and the wilder the towns. At one of these upcountry outposts, a crowd of Muslim men were singing and clapping their hands and bouncing up and down like pistons. A few of them carried a local sheik on their shoulders. Some took advantage of the holy day to fire off their guns—which only the day before we had been told were illegal to own.

The bus climbed into Ethiopia's semiarid highlands where *chaat*, an important cash crop, grows in abundance. *Chaat* is exported to Somalia, Djibouti, Yemen, and even as far away as the U.K., USA, and Canada. While Muslims eschew alcohol, this mildly mind-altering substance is considered perfectly acceptable. The Islamic clergy has been known to call it the "food of the pious." Users defend its harmlessness, but Muslim men throughout the Horn of Africa do a mean impression of *chaat* addicts. Our fellow bus passengers eagerly purchased bundles of the greens and passed clumps back and forth across the seats. Once a sleepy bunch, they suddenly became talkative and interactive. Sarah chewed on a stem to the delight of other passengers.

At Dire Dawa we transferred from the large overland bus to a minibus that regularly plied the thirty-mile (fifty-five kilometer) route from Dire Dawa to Harar. The police stopped our minibus on the outskirts of Dire Dawa. An officer peered inside, slightly bobbing his head while counting the number of passengers. I smiled, thinking that perhaps a happy foreigner would make the policeman extend extra good will. No such luck. He handed the driver a ticket for overcrowding, although no one was ordered to get off the bus. The driver's response was muted. He simply crammed more people into the vehicle as we got farther away from authority and closer to Harar, making up for the financial loss of the ticket.

Speeding along the Dire Dawa to Harar road, the minibus skirted the Rift Valley escarpment and sailed down a majestic wide avenue bordered by massive eucalyptus trees. The land was luxuriant, like the Kenyan highlands, but not quite as green. Our guidebook, which by now we threatened to throw under the wheels of the van, called this one of the most scenic drives in the world. To be fair, I would place it near the top, but several drives through the Western Cape Province of South Africa could put this one to shame.

A receptionist donning Coke-bottle lens eyeglasses greeted us at the private Belaynesh Hotel.

"It must come with the job," remarked Sarah. She recounted the hiring process: "You will be paid a competitive salary and assigned a pair of thick, black-rimmed glasses. Congratulations."

The receptionist garbled his words in an unusual manner. He sounded like I imagine Americans must sound to foreigners—as if we have a handful of marbles in our mouth.

In our room we found a few sheets of toilet paper folded neatly and placed beside the toilet. In Ethiopia there was an endless need for toilet paper, both for its intended use and to blow your nose, which runs constantly due to all the dust in the air. We asked the bespectacled clerk if we might be allocated some more. This request made no impact. After a long discussion we discovered that the Ethiopian-English term for this commodity was "soft."

"Soft!" we cooed. "Could we have some more soft?"

We were handed another folded ration.

Harar, with its ninety-nine mosques, was Islam's fourth holiest city after Mecca, Medina, and Jerusalem. From the hotel balcony, the view of the medieval walled city was inspiring. The evening sun's golden rays rippled across the rooftops. One building was capped with a tearoom, as I had seen in Zanzibar. Beyond the city limits, valleys and mountains stretched into the horizon for endless miles. Sarah and I imagined, inaccurately, that we could see as far as Somalia. Actually, we were looking into the Ogaden, a triangle of barren land owned by Ethiopia but claimed by Somalia, and thus the site of intermittent military conflict since 1961.

Several guidebooks warned that it was easy to get lost in the windy streets of the old walled city of Harar and that people could be aggressive towards foreigners. The nineteenth-century English explorer Richard Burton made the Harari xenophobic legacy famous. "A tradition exists," Burton wrote, "that with the entrance of the first Christian Harar will fall. All therefore who have attempted it were murdered." It was Burton himself who, in the 1850s, broke "the Guardian's Spell" by being the first European to enter the city and live to tell about it. Twenty years later the city was occupied by Egyptian troops.

The night air was cool and breezy. To start with, Sarah and I decided to wander through the newer, European-style section of the city, gathering up nerve to enter the old town. Under the shield of darkness, we could spot the lunatics before they spotted us and were able to steer clear of them. Figuring things could not get much worse than in Lalibela, we passed through one of the grand archways and entered medieval Harar.

The main thoroughfare hummed with people and was lined, to our surprise, with bar after bar. Zairian music spilled out of one dark doorway as two bodies gyrated inside. Colored florescent lights hung on the sides of ancient buildings and strands of colored light-bulbs dangled across the street lending a festive air. Sarah was wearing her new purchase, a white gauze shawl with a strip of colorful hand-woven embroidery along the bottom edge. Numerous townspeople, spotting the *ferenji* wrapped in traditional Amharic cloth, let out good-natured laughs and called out towards her, "Blah, blah, blah, blah, blah...Amhara!"

The following morning, as the sun climbed above the walled city, the clouds were streaked in coral, tea rose, and gold. A muezzin wailed a special *Id-al-Fitr* prayer. It was the most beautiful music either of us had ever heard. With a deep, melodic voice, the crier sang in Arabic what sounded like a ballad. That defied our concept of morning muezzins who normally croaked the words *Allahu Ahkbar* (God is great) through crackling loud speakers. The exquisite voice began to fade into the background as roosters crowed, banging noises emanated from the lower floors of the hotel, and cars, trucks, and people started to shift into the streets. Peaceful moments were short-lived in Ethiopia. Flies buzzed around our heads, forcing us to rise.

Our tour guide for the day, Lishan, spoke English fairly well and was helpful. He found us a difficult pair to keep on track though. We often wandered off to peer into shops or to snap pictures of one of the world's most photogenic cities. Around each and every corner there was an irresistible splash of color—bright pastel pinks, blues, and greens radiating from decorative signs, as well as the flamboyant clothing of the populace, all set against the backdrop of pristine white-washed buildings.

Harari women's fashion was nothing short of electrifying. Females wore layered clothing, colors and patterns clashing with abandon. A sample outfit might look like this: a long shocking pink skirt over which is layered a shorter purple flounce skirt, both over shimmering emerald patterned leggings, worn with a crimson blouse, and an orange sheer head scarf fluttering in the wind. To perfect the look, a woman might don a glittering headband in blue, green, or silver, or draw a beauty mark on her face. The motto of this hodgepodge style? Rules about matching colors, patterns, and fabrics be damned!

Harar, a cultural crossroads town, was vaunted by local residents as a happy mix of Christian and Muslim peoples from many different tribes. One can hear Somali, Arabic, Amharic, Oromo, Tigrinya, and Harari (Adare) spoken on the streets. Certainly, the preponderance of bars filling retail space in the walled

*Ethiopia is a multi-lingual country; a sign in Arabic, Amharic, and Oromia in Harar town*

city's main street and the public way so many people smoked cigarettes spoke volumes for the liberal nature of the community.

The most recent Ethiopian census found Harari regional state to have a population of 139,000, many of whom resided in the town. But African census figures are notoriously low. For instance, that same census claimed the population of Addis Ababa was only 2.3 million, whereas other sources estimate twice that number. Where the census proves more useful is in its ethnic breakdown. For example, it shows that about fifty percent of the population in Harari state are Oromo, thirty-two percent are Amhara, seven percent Harari, and three percent Gurage. Of these people, sixty percent are Muslim and thirty-eight percent Christian.

Upon seeing Sarah and me, children excitedly sang out, "*Ferenji! Ferenji!*" Our presence elicited several "I love you's" from young girls and grown men alike. Some tots called out, "Biro, pen!" Our response to this latter call was to wag our fingers at their frowning faces and say, "No, that's bad." We kidded ourselves into thinking we might actually have some influence on the cessation of this disagreeable habit. As was so common in Eritrea, and so uncommon along Ethiopia's historic route, several adults steered youthful nuisances out of our path.

I asked Lishan why there were so many crazy people in Harar.

"It's because of *chaat*," he replied matter-of-factly.

That was not a very scientific answer, considering that we had seen mad people all over that country, even where *chaat* wasn't being chewed. We saw only two other foreigners during our visit to Harar. Sarah and I asked Lishan and several other sources whether many tourists come to the town.

"Oh yes, many!" was the standard reply.

"Then why are we the only ones here?" said Sarah or I, pressing the point.

And the reply, "Because it is the end of the tourist season." While we thought we'd been blazing a trail, according to the locals we had simply missed high season.

A popular activity for tourists in Harar, Sarah and I had heard, was to watch the hyena men. These curious men charged spectators a fee to watch them feed wild hyenas outside the Old City Wall. The sheer peculiarity of this event coaxed us into wanting to experience it for ourselves. But no one could tell us where the spectacle was supposed to take place. A worker at the Belaynesh Hotel informed us that we would have to prearrange a special presentation. We decided against this plan, both because of the high fee quoted and because of the uncomfortable thought of what we imagined to be an indigent old man tossing offal and bones at wild animals at some risk to life and limb for the mere amusement of two travelers. Later, I read that the hyena men of Harar were quite popular with tourists in the 1970s but were now virtually a thing of the past. "The band of hyena men," informed the guidebook, "has been reduced to one aging nutter." But both *Africa A to Z* dated 1961 and 1972 and *The*

*Traveler's Africa* from 1973 speak of only one nameless Hyena Man, so I suspect it was always a case of "one aging nutter."

We also had intentions of purchasing the distinctive Harari baskets, like those we saw hanging on the walls of a Canadian expatriate's house in Addis Ababa. Harari baskets are flat and round, usually in rich red shades, and often with cowrie shells secured to the ends of four leather straps dangling over the edges. Our tour guide took us to several private homes where they sold large collections of these baskets, as well as other traditional artifacts. The Harari people know all too well the value of these antiques to foreigners. The prices, starting at around US $50 for old baskets, were incredibly high for Africa. Tour guides must have received a cut of this price, because both the home-owners and Lishan looked terribly disappointed when we didn't buy anything. However, this "window-shopping" did allow us to peak into a few private households. Both of the two-story buildings were constructed around inner courtyards. One had an ingenious contraption—a string attached from the courtyard door handle up to the second-floor balcony so that residents could open the door without having to run downstairs.

Another tourist staple is the home of the famous nineteenth-century French poet Jean Nicholas Arthur Rimbaud, who in the latter years of his short life was a trader and gunrunner in Africa. The house was in a state of collapse, but restoration work was underway. With its lacy wooden facade, the dilapidated home sits on a hill overlooking a small mosque and corrugated tin-roofed buildings. The entryway's cement rails were crumbling. Looking two stories up, we saw a painted canvas ceiling that tells a bucolic tale of seas, country bridges and stone buildings, but the canvas draped downward where it had torn away from the rafters. A cool breeze streamed in through open colored-glass windows in the second-story room, from where we could see the endless horizon surrounding Harar.

*Inside "Rimbaud's" house in Harar*

Our guidebook claimed that Ethiopians erro-
neously call this house Rimbaud's, and that, in fact,
the poet lived elsewhere. We proffered this comment to
our guide.

"No," he insisted. "Rimbaud did live here."

"Maybe he owned it," I suggested. "But didn't actually live here."

Our guide and the house's guardian both maintained that it was indeed Rimbaud's house. They proceeded to recount the story of Rimbaud's descent into
madness after his Ethiopian wife left him, and of his
flight into the desert, travelling on foot to Djibouti.

I had read that Rimbaud's love interest at the end
of his life was not a fair Ethiopian maiden, but rather
a young servant boy. Fearing the guardian's surely
indignant response, I decided, as they say in America,
not to go there. While I wasn't even aware of it at the
time, there is one damning piece of evidence that could
foil this house's future as a tourist attraction: Rimbaud
died in 1891 and the house was built at the turn of the
century. I wondered how the Ethiopian government,

having sunk a tidy sum of money into the Rimbaud House restoration, would deal with these contradictions when better informed and less culturally sensitive tourists started streaming through. According to the Ethiopian News Agency (ENA), already 2,400 foreign and local tourists visit Rimbaud's house each year.

Whatever the details of the Rimbaud story, the house is a romantic reminder of a not too distant past and, therefore, constitutes a worthy stop on any tourist itinerary.

*   *   *

Flying back to Addis Ababa seemed a more prudent course of action than retracing the tracks of our long, sticky bus journey. We returned to Dire Dawa to catch an Ethiopian Airlines flight back to the capital. The new Sai Hotel in Dire Dawa was clean and comfortable, and we were happy to have chosen it. There was only one catch. Because they cater to a Muslim clientele—a Saudi Airlines agent's office is stationed in the lobby—they don't serve alcohol. In the miniature refrigerator in our hotel room we discovered all the refreshing Harar-produced Babile mineral water that we could want. But, being denied beer, we craved it madly.

"Where is a popular place to go at night?" I inquired at the front desk.

"The Ras Hotel," was the unqualified answer.

The Ras Hotel was the government-owned hotel that had been bombed only two weeks before, purportedly by a Somali separatist movement. Sarah and I entered the Ras lobby. It looked as if a wicked witch had, thirty years earlier, cast a time freezing spell. This being so, it would have meant the hotel had been bewitched for a large part of the city's existence: Dire Dawa was built less than a century earlier as the headquarters for the French while constructing the 547 mile (880 kilometer) long Addis Ababa to Djibouti narrow-gauge rail line.

It appeared the evil spell had recently been lifted, and the staff stood around waiting for the clocks to start ticking again. The furnishings, right up to the ceiling fixtures, were straight out of the 1960s. We noticed earlier in the day other relics from the sixties in Dire Dawa town. In a cafe facing the train station stood a burger boy statue similar to Frisch's *Big Boy*. Other cafes were fenced off with metal grills decorated with geometric shapes in primary colors.

There was no one, but no one, at the Ras Hotel. A waiter politely escorted us out the back door, through the unused pool grounds, to a poolside bar. The music in the bar blared eerily out of proportion, considering there was not one customer. The waiter turned to resume his watch inside the morgue. Sarah and I just continued out into the street, laughing at the thought that the one pair of customers the Ras Hotel had received in thirty years was officially escorted right through the back door and into the street. It was early yet, however, and we knew that this part of the world began its nightlife very late.

Not far from the Ras Hotel was a small bar. We entered with intentions of satisfying our newly found obsession with beer. The owner was a short, light-skinned European-looking man. His wife, a large woman with a cloudy eye, was unmistakably African. We inquired about food. They did not have any injera ready, but urged us to come back the next day for lunch.

"But we have to catch a plane to Addis at ten in the morning," I protested.

Both of them laughed.

"Oh, they are always delayed," the man said. "Maybe one o'clock or so. They tell you ten, but one o'clock. You come back tomorrow for food."

As we were leaving the bar, with a fuzzy feeling after consuming two beers and no dinner, the little man warned us, "Be careful of thieves." Sarah and I walked through the dark streets babbling about violent crime in Nairobi. We chuckled, speculating about what could possibly have been Dire Dawa's version of crime and how easily we'd become tipsy.

A young woman on the street pointed, and using the Italian word for car, told us there was an open-air restaurant near the *macchina*. We settled into a table on the veranda and were served *shiro* (mashed lentils and chickpeas) and *gomen* (cooked green vegetables). Both tasted decidedly spicier than food in Eritrea. Sarah and I had been long-time fans of Ethiopian food from our years living in Kenya. The statement made in D.J. Mesfin's book *Exotic Ethiopian Cooking* was accurate indeed: "Once hooked, it's for life."

There were only a few other customers in the restaurant. Mostly our view was of empty tables and chairs strewn in the garden under the blackness of night. I was determined to discover the hidden side of this city—we had to be missing something. So I queried the waiter about a place I usually prefer to avoid.

"Is there a disco?" I asked.

The waiter and the cashier looked at each other in amazement, while Sarah sat in the background having giggling fits.

"No disco in Dire Dawa," the waiter said. "Try the Ras Hotel."

\*   \*   \*

The twin gems, Harar and Dire Dawa, must be among the world's best-kept secrets.[1] The hotels and food are cheap and of relatively good quality, the natural scenery en route beautiful, the people kind and welcoming, and both places abound with history and culture. These two cities are easy to get around using blue and white taxis that for two *birr* per person

---

1. In October 1996, two foreigners were shot in broad daylight in the city of Dire Dawa. In February 1997, a grenade attack at a hotel in Harar wounded five foreigners. The U.S. State Department issued a travel warning in February 1997 advising U.S. citizens against travel to Harar and Dire Dawa. Travel to areas east and south of Harar is considered particularly dangerous because of land mines. Anyone planning a trip to Ethiopia or Eritrea should consult the State Department's traveler's advisory web page for updates. The addresses are: http://travel.state.gov/ethiopia.html and http://travel.state.gov/eritrea.html.

(equivalent to about twenty-five cents) take you any-where within the city limits. Because these are "share taxis," meaning they pick up other passengers along the way, the taxis are always busy and always avail-able. This was one of the most enjoyable public trans-portation experiences in Africa.

"Encompassed by the enemies of their religion," wrote Edward Gibbon in the *Decline and Fall of the Roman Empire*, "Aethiopians slept for near a thousand years, forgetful of the world by whom they were for-gotten." Nowadays the Ethiopians are encompassed by a world that not so much forgets, but dismisses them as just another famine-prone country of the so-called Third World. On a planet that spins by the momentum of high finance, international trade, telecommunications, and data communications, sleepy café towns like Dire Dawa that once flourished under a lingering empire are left in the silicon chip dust.

\* \* \*

It had turned ten o'clock. The town was wrapped in a lovely enveloping warmth. Maybe, just maybe, the Ras Hotel would be swinging by then. When we got there, however, the atmosphere could only be described as funereal. Dire Dawa was a clean, modern, European-style city. The people we met were friendly and relaxed. The weather was dry and warm. But at night, and much of the day, its wide streets lined with shade trees more so than not resembled a ghost town. The city had a population of approximately 100,000 people, but the question Sarah and I repeatedly asked each other was this: "Where is everybody?"

It wasn't always like this. In his book *Sheba Slept Here*, Alan Caillou, a police chief of the area following World War II when the British administered parts of Ethiopia, wrote of Dire Dawa:

There was a cacophony of European languages coming from the terraces. A cinema poster was advertising *Le Jour*

245

*Se Leve*, with Jean Gabin and Arletty....Even though the
majority of people on the streets were Ethiopian....the
flavor was still....of Paris, with a touch of Italian resorts
thrown in for good measure. There were advertisements for
Cinzano everywhere, and Marie Brizard, and Gomme
Pirelli, and Parfums Lavin, and all the nostalgic products
that seemed to reflect a prewar Europe, where people sat
in pavement cafes, just as they did here....

The diminutive bar owner had confirmed that before
the Mengistu regime took over the country, there were
in fact many Greeks, Italians, and French living in Dire
Dawa. Now the city was like a caller on long hold, a
place waiting for an international community to come
back, a place that in the twentieth century alone had
witnessed imperial excess, foreign administration, and
communist frugality—all of which sent shivers of terror
through the spine of the country. Dire Dawa was a
place wondering what it would become, and moreover
what its mother country would become, when it turned
the corner into a new millennium.

Like naughty schoolgirls with beer on our breath,
we wandered back to the alcohol-free Sai Hotel. We
had searched for hours throughout that attractive city
and found few signs of life. Dropping heavily onto our
beds, we still had the feeling of being schoolgirls—the
ones who weren't invited to the year's best party.

\*　\*　\*

As our taxi inched along in morning traffic on the
way to the airport, Sarah and I daydreamed about ini-
tiating an artist's colony in this city frozen-in-time. A
lunatic, his gangly body exposed under filthy scraps of
clothing, ran in front of the taxi. Facing us through
the windshield and running backwards, he began
stripping off the remainder of his tattered rags. That
was a new one—a bum flashing his bum.

Arriving at the airport at eight o'clock in the
morning, we were told the plane had been delayed.
Check-in time was bumped to noon. The bar couple

had been right. We hitched a ride on the Ethiopian Airlines bus back to town. From the bus window, we saw a crazy woman squatting in the train station square. She pointed her finger rigidly at passing cars and berated them individually, I suppose for their sins against God or man. As to be expected, she zeroed in on Sarah and me as we alighted from the bus, and followed us all the while pointing and mumbling angry sentiments.

The dividing line between Kezira, the section of Dire Dawa distinguished by its European architecture, and Megala, the local, more Arabic-style quarters, was a *lagga*, a wide, dry riverbed. In Alan Caillou's day this river bed had been cordoned off by rolls of barbed wire, separating the Europeans from the locals and vice versa. Today, Sarah and I casually wandered across the *lagga*. A deformed man with feet turned backward hobbled across the dirt supporting himself with a cane. A little girl walked between Sarah and me with hands outstretched in order to touch both of us on the legs and continued silently on her way. Although the *ferenji* were definitely taken note of, residents of southeastern Ethiopia seemed less aggressive, less hungry for attention and *birr*. There was a large market on the local side of the riverbed. Brilliantly colored cloth and clothing hung in permanent stalls, along with other bits and pieces useful for daily life. The market was not necessarily bustling, just motoring along, like Dire Dawa itself.

Shaded outdoor cafés were plentiful in the European section of Dire Dawa, but they served no fresh juices, only sodas, tea, and coffee, and food seemed particularly hard to come by. At the Banker's Café it took me several minutes to arrange for a fried egg sandwich. This leafy restaurant was completely empty with the exception of one congenial, elderly man who assured us that at around one o'clock in the afternoon and later in the evening the place became busy. He was quick to engage us in conversation about Ethiopia.

"I'm one hundred percent sure," the man said of his hopes that the country would change for the better. Like others before him, he praised the days of Haile Selassie and in a low voice, surely out of habit, informed us that Ethiopia's real problems started with the Derg. "This government is not yet democratic fully," he said, "but it is better than the one before. We need investment. Handouts are not good. We need jobs. I can work, but there are no jobs. There is much hunger and illness."

The man informed us with pride that he was trained as an airplane mechanic by the Americans. During Selassie's days, American consultants managed Ethiopian Airlines, held key posts in the emperor's ministries, and provided training to the military. These days, the United States is scheduled to donate US$ 50 million in food aid over the next three years (1996-1998), making Ethiopia third on the list of African countries receiving U.S. aid.

"I think you are American," the man said to me with a touch of fondness. Then he apologized, "I talk too much." In a cloud of melancholy, he returned to his table.

# Departure

*A conversation with a
friend and a proverb
from an old lady; while
interesting, one must
leave them.*

— Oromo proverb

It was Orthodox Lent. Throughout
Addis Ababa, churchyards overflowed with parishioners soberly
absorbing sermons. About half of
Ethiopia's population belongs to the
Ethiopian Orthodox Church, an indigenous Christian church. Like Jews and
Muslims—with whom Ethiopians also
share linguistic affinities—Orthodox
Ethiopians do not eat pork. Lent, a six-
week prelude to Easter, is marked by
increased attendance at church as well
as by a period of austerity and fasting.
Strict adherents live only on water and
unleavened bread, the latter made
palatable with spices. Those who
violate Lenten rules, according to
Orthodox commandments, will smell of
"hellish sulfur."

Fasting food is a great Ethiopian oxymoron. For Muslims, fasting during the holy month of Ramadan requires abstaining from eating a single bite of food or drinking a drop of liquid while the sun is up. Feasting begins at sundown. For Orthodox Christians, fasting involves abstaining from eating any animal or bird product, including milk, eggs, butter, and cheese. From what Sarah and I observed, however, there was certainly no ban on vegetables, and I mean heaps of them.

"Actually," Tesfaye had explained earlier, "they become vegens."

Orthodox Ethiopians who consider themselves sinners pray outside the church, while those considering themselves pure may go inside. To remain pure, one must behave properly and fast for the two months of Lent and Easter, as well as fast every Wednesday and Friday throughout the year. That's a grand total of 165 fasting days, or nearly half the year. No wonder so many of the laity were praying outside the churches. Nonetheless, the air in the church court-yards was fresh and thin, smelling nothing like sulphur.

Sarah and I made a last-ditch effort to be good tourists and found our way to Saint George's Cathedral. The Cathedral, located near the Piazza, held a commanding view over the city and of the mountains beyond. No other site in Addis adequately evoked the feeling of being in the world's fourth highest capital city. Saint George's was built in 1896 to commemorate Ethiopia's victory over Italy at the Battle of Adowa. A much revered historical event in Ethiopia, Adowa not only marks the first time that an African army routed a European force, it also stands as an annual reminder that Ethiopia was the only African country that was never colonized.

As expected, beggars lined the Cathedral's perime-ter walls hoping for crumbs of compassion from the faithful during the sacred season. Women entered the compound gate, made a low bow, and repeatedly crossed themselves. Men approached the octagonal building and kissed the stone walls several times. While plenty of verdant trees grew inside the cathedral compound, the ground below them was nothing but dirt and rubble. The devout—mostly middle-aged women—settled on rocks, cement blocks, and steps, listening to the sermon being blasted over a loud speaker. The priest held a tattered multicolored umbrella over his head while he read the sermon, I'd venture to say in Ge'ez, the liturgical language.

In Eritrea, Rachel had told me that Ethiopia's *Timket* (Epiphany) ceremonies, and the priests officiating them, seemed, to her anyway, less than holy. Margery Perham, in her book *The Government of Ethiopia*, also commented on this, saying that Ethiopian lives were "pervaded by religion without being really spiritual." I, too, concluded that the priests I'd seen appeared about as spiritual as my mailman and went about their jobs with much less enthusiasm.

It seemed to me that the women of Ethiopia expressed the greatest reverence for their church and their God. Perhaps they were the spiritual core of this country more so than the dime-a-dozen priests and monks. It was the women who dominated the churchyards during this Lenten season; it was the women who pulled their white gauzy shawls over their heads and mouths in poses of deep pious contemplation; it was the women about whom sons complained for being too god-fearing, mocking them for tending to daily religious duties.

\* \* \*

Sarah and I finally managed to both be healthy and energetic enough while in Addis Ababa to splurge on a big night out. Our first stop was the five-star Addis Ababa Hilton Hotel for a cocktail. Sarah came along kicking and scratching. She reckoned the Hilton Hotel was symbolic of carbon-copy societies and, worse yet, was a bastion of the operatives of Third World exploitation. Once inside the hotel's peaceful walls, however, and after being served a few tasty complimentary

snacks and a chilled beer while surrounded by impec-
cably-dressed businessmen at the hot-springs poolside bar, she succumbed to its snobbish charms.

Outside the Hilton, we walked past a short, stocky
kid with dreadlocks. He had a strong Jamaican accent
and a grown-up manner that made me glance twice
to be sure he wasn't a midget. The boy touted the
reggae nightclub in front of which he stood. This juvenile street tout was likely the offspring of Jamaican
Rastafarians who came to Ethiopia during the Selassie
era. Rastafarians worshipped Haile Selassie, who
before becoming Emperor was known as *Ras* Tafari.
(*Ras* an Ethiopian title of nobility, literally means
"head" and is equivalent to the European title duke.)

In the dark, Addis Ababa loses its grayish-blue tint
ascribed by the city's prodigious eucalyptus trees. It is
these sturdy Australian imports that give Addis its
steely, drippy tenor. After the turn of the century,
Emperor Menelik II, facing a fuelwood and construction material shortage in his new capital was considering moving the capital. It had been the pattern for
Ethiopian capital cities to move when wood resources
became exhausted. Instead, Menelik II ordered all residents to plant a fast-growing eucalyptus tree beside
their house. By the 1920s, Addis Ababa became
known as Eucalyptopolis. These slender towering trees
are well-established denizens of Addis Ababa nowadays.

We ate dinner at the Ibex Hotel, a popular spot to
indulge in national cuisine while watching traditional
Ethiopian dancers. The dancers jerked their bodies
around in a most impressive manner. Sweat poured
down their faces as they shimmied their shoulders and
wiggled their necks like ostriches. One male dancer
could vibrate his entire body like a jackhammer. A
woman dancer's breasts popped up and down and
circled around, I kid you not, in opposite directions.
The band, dressed in crisp white outfits, were the spitting image of the pictures of traditional bands painted
on animal hides and sold at tourist shops. One man
played a drum, one a flute, another a banjo-like instru-

ment called a *kirar*, and the last played something roughly resembling a violin.

Most of the customers, aside from a spattering of foreigners, were well-to-do Ethiopians. We compared the composition of this crowd to one in a similar setting in Kenya's capital, Nairobi, where the patrons in many of the finer restaurants were almost exclusively European or Asian. There certainly were indigenous Kenyans with money, but they didn't often spend it on fine dining. From this and other observations— the sophisticated sense of humor and the predilection for café life encountered in Eritrea and Dire Dawa—I deduced that Ethiopians and Eritreans have sensibilities about what to do with their expendable income and leisure time that are more akin to Europeans than to other Africans.

The popular Torero bar across the street was, like many places in the capital, a converted house. The Gypsy Kings playing on the stereo matched the Spanish bullfighter theme. The smokey bar quickly filled with upper crust Ethiopians, expats, and difficult-to-place ethnic mixtures. Sarah and I didn't have quite as much stamina as we had hoped and, after a beer, walked back into the dark street to hail a cab. As we had come to expect, the cab drivers waiting outside the bars and restaurants in this busy area tried to rip us off, but this time it was royally.

"It is late at night," one taxi driver said in justification of the skyrocketed price.

Sarah and I were too tired to argue, so we called their bluff and proceeded on the long walk home. We were absolutely sure that one of the drivers, who did in fact want to make a few *birr* and who wasn't driven by the untenable need to make a stupendous profit from tourists, would break away from the pack. We were right.

\* \* \*

Mid-morning, Sarah burst into our room at the Holiday Hotel.

"It's amazing how much can happen in a short time!" she bubbled.

Sarah had gone into town for one hour. She encountered a gang of streetboys practicing pickpocket techniques. One pulled her arm to divert her attention, while a few others made a feeble attempt at grabbing her backpack.

"It was pathetic really," she scoffed. "Amateurs."

On one minibus the tout had tried to overcharge her; she reported giving him a thorough reaming. While on another, the entire bus struck up a conversation with her and several of the passengers invited her to visit their upcountry homes. After that, she managed to drop a few hundred dollars for silver jewelry and a religious icon.

Locals and expatriates alike had been quick to warn us about pickpockets in Addis—with good reason. In our incursions into the city's unruly streets, we were, on two occasions, the victims of aspiring pickpockets. The first time, as we walked along a crowded sidewalk, a young boy moved close to me. When I turned my head away, he flicked aside my neck scarf hoping to find a necklace worth snatching. He was disappointed. Sarah and I had just bought local crosses, pieces of leather and scrap metal hung on black string that are sold on the streets for two *birr*. The second time was Sarah's backpack incident, mentioned above.

While pickpockets may be rampant, more egregious crimes appeared to be kept to a minimum. I asked one expatriate about house break-ins.

"Well, yes." she said, "They happen. A house in our neighborhood was robbed, oh, one or two years ago."

Nairobi residents would surely roar with laughter at the innocence of her statement. Most people living in Nairobi could list several burglaries in their neighborhood, sometimes with violence, and many occurring in the recent past. Carjackings, another Nairobi specialty, was reportedly uncommon in Ethiopia, most cases occurring in remote areas where bandits, known as *shifta*, operated.

"In our neighborhood," explained the expat, "everyone knows who you are, whether you know them or not."

I joined Sarah for a last round in the streets of Addis Ababa. A teenage boy followed us up Churchill Road, sputtering the usual tiring spate of questions:

"Where are you from? What is your work? Where are you going?"

To which Sarah's response was, "It really doesn't matter."

The boy persisted with the same line of questioning, so Sarah attempted reason.

"You know," she explained, "everyone we meet asks us the same questions over and over again. We are sick of it and would really like to be left to walk alone."

"But," he replied, "I want to practice my English." Another unshakable one.

Still working on reason, I replied, "We don't want to practice English. We are not English teachers."

The teenager dropped back a bit and yelled, "African bloodsuckers. Mother Fucker."

That was it. I'd had it with this kid and this country too. I whipped around, fire in my eyes, and stormed down the sidewalk after him. The street vendors looked on with mild curiosity as the boy quickly dropped his angry epithets and backed down the street, pursued by a crazed *ferenji*. Just as I was preparing to leave, I finally developed the skills necessary to confront this strange land. Should I have stayed much longer—a frightful thought—perhaps I, too, would have been caught throwing jabs and punches on busy street corners.

\* \* \*

Long ago, according to Oden Meeker in *Report on Africa*, "informed circles in Europe were mainly aware that the Ethiopians were men without heads, and ate the flesh of dragons to cool themselves in the summer." In *The Africans*, David Lamb reminded us that during Homeric times Ethiopians were known as "the farthest away of all mankind," and that "their country was supposed to be the place where the sun set." Ethiopian public relations were further harmed by their emperors' penchant for forbidding foreign travelers from ever leaving.

I felt fairly certain that no one as eminent as an emperor knew of our arrival in the Land of Perennial Spring, and just as confident that none would prevent our departure. The taxi driver who took Sarah and me the five miles to Bole Airport was Eritrean. Not unlike other locals I had met both there and in Eritrea, he announced that he had relatives living abroad—six brothers in London.

"Ethiopia has good land," the taxi driver said in broken English, "but not good people. I love Eritrea for the people. They are clean and friendly. Just like Europeans." Pushing through the unruly traffic, he continued, "Here, when they argue with you they'll say, 'What are you doing here anyway? It's not your country.' "

In 1955, in his book *Inside Africa*, John Gunther called Ethiopia "both blessed and tortured," and I have to agree. Ethiopia is the epitome of the hackneyed adage "Africa is a land of contrasts." There are glaring geographic and climatic contrasts: a 15,000-foot mountain with corresponding cool climes (even snowfall at times) versus lowlands that must feel like the interior of a woodburning stove. Ethiopia is destitute beyond description, yet possesses near mythic beauty, both in its landscape and in its citizenry. The country flings obstacles and annoyances at the visitor at every turn, all the while presenting remarkable historical treasures and unforgettable niches of paradise.

Despite my many grievances, I felt enriched for having traveled there, if only in the way one feels fortified after having completed some physical test of endurance, like climbing a mountain or crossing a marathon finish line. Before coming to Ethiopia, I had already been smitten by the trappings of the country's culture—the elaborately spiced foods, the comfortable cotton clothing with its vibrant borders, the unrefined

silver jewelry and peculiarly yellow gold, the mesmer-
izing music, the sumptuous history, and the gracious
manners and serene smiles of earth's most comely
people.

Soon enough I'll disregard the manifold headaches
and hassles, and, once again, Ethiopia's captivating
traits will rise above all else. Few would say that
Ethiopia is easy. Perhaps I am an optimist, perhaps a
fool, but I can envision an Ethiopia—like the continent of which it is part—restored one day to its right-
ful status as a land of greatness.

The taxi drove past a mad woman sitting along the
roadside with her legs splayed out in the dirt. In front
of her feet she had built a miniature twig shrine. She
sang and clapped deliriously. I sensed the woman had
been stationed there by some higher power to bid us
a final goodbye. Her whole being seemed to wail:
farewell, from the land of mystery and magic.

*I saw parch'd Abyssinia rouse and sing.*

— John Keats (1795-1821)

# Postscript

In May 1997, I received the following message from Sarah in an e-mail entitled "Was it you?"

*Just reading a snippet about the Lalibela Cross having disappeared—presumed stolen—from the depths of Medhane Alem. Mmm, very strange. It was last seen sometime around February 1996.... Says here that after the discovery of the theft the whole town of Lalibela was transformed into a "wailing mass of villagers, priests and nuns, beating their breasts, tearing out their hair and calling on God to rescue them." Obviously what this reporter didn't know was that this is actually the normal course of the day in Lalibela. Should we tell them?*

*Are you coming to the wedding?*

# Bibliography

**BOOKS**

Allen, Philip M. and Aaron Segal. *The Traveler's Africa.* New York: Hopkinson and Blake, 1973.

Connell, Dan. *Against All Odds.* Trenton, New Jersey: Red Sea Press, 1993.

Gunther, John. *Inside Africa.* New York: Harper & Brothers, 1955.

Iyob, Ruth. *The Eritrean Struggle for Independence.* New York: Cambridge University Press, 1995.

Kapuscinski, Ryszard. *The Emperor: Downfall of an Autocrat.* New York: Harcourt Brace Jovanovich, 1978 (English translation 1983).

Keneally, Thomas. *To Asmara.* New York: Warner Books, 1989.

Lamb, David. *The Africans.* London: Methuen Paperback, 1985.

Meeker, Oden. *Report on Africa.* New York: Charles Scribner's Sons, 1954.

Papstein, Robert. *Eritrea, Revolution at Dusk.* New Jersey: The Red Sea Press, 1991.

Pateman, Roy. *Eritrea, Even the Stones Are Burning.* New Jersey: Red Sea Press, 1990.

Perham, Margery. *The Government of Ethiopia.*

Pye-Smith, Charlie. *The Other Nile.* New York: Penguin Books, 1986.

Sherman, Richard. *Eritrea: The Unfinished Revolution.* New York: Praeger, 1980. (I am particularly indebted to this book for historical background.)

Woodward, Peter and Murray Forsyth. *Conflict and Peace in the Horn of Africa.* England: Dartmouth Publishing Company, 1994.

Yohannes, Okbazghi. *Eritrea: A Pawn in World Politics* Gainesville: University of Florida Press, 1991.

## ARTICLES AND JOURNALS

"Eritrea: Independence Declared." *Facts on File World News Digest,* May 27, 1993, p. 397.

*Horn of Africa Bulletin,* July-August 1996, Life & Peace Institute, Uppsala, Sweden.

Jalata, Asafa. "The Struggle for Knowledge: The Case of Emergent Oromo Studies," *African Studies Review,* September 1996, pp. 95-123.

Kaplan, Robert D. "New World Orphan: Eritrea's Sudden Rebirth." *The New Republic,* June 24, 1991, p. 16.

Michaels, Marguerite. "Horn of Africa: Tough Terms for a Divorce." *Time,* July 15, 1991, p. 34.

Rude, John C., *The Humanist,* March-April 1996, p. 17.

"The Birth of a Nation in Cyberspace." *The Humanist,* March-April 1996.


## WEB SITES

*CIA World Factbooks*
  www.odci.gov/cia/publications/factbook
*Eritrea Community Online - Dehai*
  www.dehai.org
*Eritrea Network Information Center*
  www.eritrea.org
*Ethiopian Jewish Foods and Recipes*
  www.circus.org//13.html
*FAOSTAT Database*
  apps.fao.org
*Lycos City Guides*
  cityguide.lycos.com
*Peace Corps Country Information*
  www.peacecorps.gov/www/dp/fact/WWSEritrea.html
  www.peacecorps.gov/www/dp/fact/WWSEthiopia.html
*State of Ethiopia's Children 1995*
  198.76.84.1/HORN/ethiopia/UNICEF/ethiopia.html
*U.S. Department of State Country Reports on Human Rights Practices*
  www.state.gov/www/global/human_rights/hrp_reports_mainhp.html

*WHO Database*
www.who.ch/hst/hsp/a/countrys/eri3.htm
www.who.ch/hst/hsp/a/countrys/eth3.htm
*World Bank Press Releases*
www.worldbank.org/html/extdr/extme/press.html

# Index